THE CROONER

The Art of Crooning and the Timeless Legacy of Tony Bennett

Wayne Devlin BCAa

Kindle Direct Publishing

Copyright © 2024 Wayne Devlin BCAa

All rights reserved

This book is not endorsed by, affiliated with, or associated with the estate of Tony Bennett. It reflects solely the author's personal views and serves as a tribute to the life and legacy of Tony Bennett.

No part of this book may be reproduced, or stored in a retrieval system, or transmitted in any form or by any means, electronic, mechanical, photocopying, recording, or otherwise, without express written permission of the publisher.

Cover Photograph: Wayne Devlin
Printed in the United Kingdom

To the memory of Tony Bennett, a true master of the art of crooning. Your voice, your grace, and your unwavering commitment to the music have left an indelible mark on the hearts of millions. You showed us the power of sincerity, the beauty of storytelling through song, and the timelessness of love and connection. Your legacy will forever inspire generations of singers and listeners alike.

Thank you for the music, the memories, and the gift of your voice. You will always be remembered.

"I've been very fortunate that I've been able to sing as long as I have, and I enjoy singing now more than I did when I first started."
— Tony Bennett

These words remind us that passion, dedication, and love for the craft never fade. Tony Bennett's voice continues to echo through time, a testament to the beauty of perseverance and the lasting power of music.

TONY BENNETT

CONTENTS

Title Page
Copyright
Dedication
Epigraph
Foreword
Introduction
Preface
Prologue

Chapter 1: The Birth of Crooning	1
Chapter 2: Bing Crosby and the Early Pioneers	5
Chapter 3: Frank Sinatra and the Crooner as a Cultural Icon	9
Chapter 4: The Golden Age of Radio and Television	13
Chapter 5: Tony Bennett's Journey	18
Chapter 6: My Story Begins: Discovering Crooning	22
Chapter 7: The Las Vegas Dream: A Near Chance with Tony Bennett	26
Chapter 8: The Global Impact of Crooning	30
Chapter 9: Nat King Cole and the Art of Smooth Singing	35
Chapter 10: The Evolution of Crooning in Modern Music	40
Chapter 11: Meeting Tony Bennett in Manchester	45
Chapter 12: The Alzheimer's Fundraiser: Singing for 24	50

Hours

Chapter 13: Tony Bennett's Response: A Personal Thank You — 57

Chapter 14: The Women of Crooning — 62

Chapter 15: The Decline of Crooning in the 1970s and 1980s — 67

Chapter 16: The Revival of Crooning: From Harry Connick Jr. to Michael Bublé — 72

Chapter 17: The Craft of Crooning: Technique and Mastery — 77

Chapter 18: The Emotional Core of Crooning — 83

Chapter 19: Crooning's Cultural Impact: Elegance, Romance, and Cool — 88

Chapter 20: The Art of Live Performance: Crooning in the Moment — 93

Chapter 21: Crooning's Influence on Modern Genres — 98

Chapter 22: The Timeless Legacy of Tony Bennett — 103

Chapter 23: Crooning in the Digital Age — 108

Chapter 24: The Future of Crooning: Carrying the Tradition Forward — 113

Chapter 25: Crooning's Enduring Legacy — 118

Epilogue — 123

Afterword — 125

Acknowledgement — 129

About The Author — 131

133

FOREWORD

When I sit and think about crooning, I think about the voices that have shaped not just music, but moments in our lives. Crooning is more than a style of singing, it's an emotional connection, a way of turning simple melodies into something deeply personal and intimate. For decades, it has provided the soundtrack to love, heartache, hope, and nostalgia. At the forefront of this tradition stands Tony Bennett, a man whose voice has moved generations and whose legacy continues to inspire singers, just like me.

I didn't grow up in the age of the big band orchestras, but the sound of crooning, specifically Tony Bennett's voice, still found its way into my life. His music had a timeless quality that resonated deeply, no matter the era. Even when modern trends dominated the charts, there was something comforting and familiar about the classic sound of Tony's smooth vocals. Whether he was singing I Left My Heart in San Francisco or effortlessly gliding through the jazz standards, Tony made every song feel like a personal conversation between him and the listener.

Tony Bennett's career, spanning more than seven decades, is a testament to the power of passion, perseverance, and authenticity. He didn't chase fame or trends, he remained steadfast in his love for the Great American Songbook, and in doing so, he kept those songs alive for new generations. He showed that music, when sung from the heart, can transcend time. Tony was a crooner in the truest sense of the word, someone who could make you feel something real, simply through the warmth of his voice.

In many ways, Tony Bennett's journey mirrors the evolution of crooning itself. From its beginnings in the 1920s with the advent of the microphone, crooning has always been about intimacy and nuance. It allowed singers to express emotion in a way that had never been possible before, and it changed the way we experience music. Tony, with his unmatched ability to convey emotion through song, became one of the greatest ambassadors of this art form.

My connection to Tony Bennett goes beyond admiration for his music. When I had the opportunity to meet him, it was a moment that solidified everything I had come to believe about the power of music to connect us. Later, after Tony revealed his battle with Alzheimer's, I felt compelled to do something in his honour. I sang for a full 24 hours to raise money for the Alzheimer's Society, and to my surprise and delight, Tony not only highlighted my efforts on his social media but personally thanked me. His words and his recognition were one of the most humbling moments of my life.

This book is not just about Tony Bennett though, it's about the art of crooning and the profound impact it has had on music and culture. It's about the voices that have shaped the tradition and the singers who continue to carry it forward today. But more than anything, it's a personal reflection on how one voice, Tony's, can leave a lasting mark on a life and how that voice becomes a bridge to something greater.

I invite you to join me on this journey through the world of crooning, where we will explore its rich history, its influence on modern music, and the lasting legacy of one of its greatest practitioners. Tony Bennett may be gone, but his voice will never be silenced. It lives on in the hearts of all who have been touched by his music, and through this book, I hope to share just a small piece of what made him, and this art form, so special.

– Wayne

Wayne Devlin BCAa

INTRODUCTION

Crooning, with its smooth melodies and heartfelt delivery, is one of the most enduring and beloved styles of singing in music history. It's a genre that transcends time, capturing the essence of human emotion in a way that few others can. From the golden age of the 1930s and 1940s, when voices like Bing Crosby and Frank Sinatra filled the airwaves, to the present day, crooning remains a symbol of romance, nostalgia, and timeless charm.

This book is a journey through the history and evolution of crooning, a vocal tradition that has touched the hearts of generations. It celebrates the voices that have defined the art form and explores how the genre has influenced modern music. Central to this story is the legacy of Tony Bennett, a true icon whose career spanned more than seven decades, proving that music, at its best, is ageless.

Tony Bennett didn't just sing songs, he lived them. His voice, rich and full of emotion, has become the soundtrack to love stories, memories, and moments of reflection. As someone who has been personally inspired by Tony's music, I have had the honour of following in his footsteps as a crooner. My own connection to Tony Bennett, from nearly singing with him in Las Vegas to fundraising in his honour for Alzheimer's research, has been one of the greatest gifts of my life. His kindness and encouragement reaffirmed for me the importance of using one's voice not only to entertain but to connect, to inspire, and to bring joy to others.

In The Crooner: The Art of Crooning and the Timeless Legacy of Tony Bennett, we'll explore the roots of crooning, its rise to prominence, and the voices that have kept it alive across generations. We'll dive into Tony Bennett's extraordinary career, tracing how he remained a central figure in music despite shifting trends and technological changes. His commitment to the Great American Songbook and his ability to collaborate with younger artists serve as proof that the beauty of crooning knows no bounds.

This book is both a tribute to Tony Bennett and an exploration of how crooning continues to thrive in today's digital age. It's a celebration of the power of music to evoke emotion, to tell stories, and to connect us all—across time, space, and generations.

So, let's embark on this journey together, honouring the great crooners of the past and looking forward to the future of an art form that will never fade.

PREFACE

The art of crooning has always held a special place in my heart. From the moment I first heard the smooth, velvety voices of the greats like Frank Sinatra, Nat King Cole, and, of course, Tony Bennett, I was captivated. There was something magical in the way they could turn a simple melody into an emotional journey, pulling the listener into a world of love, heartache, and nostalgia with nothing more than their voice and a well-placed phrase. Crooning, in its essence, is about intimacy, about the connection between the singer and the listener, about telling a story in the most heartfelt way possible.

When I began my journey as a crooner, it was these voices that guided me. I studied them, learning not only their technical prowess but their ability to express vulnerability, charm, and passion. Over time, crooning became not just a style of singing for me, but a way of life, a way of approaching music that values emotion and sincerity above all else.

In writing this book, I wanted to explore the rich history of crooning, but more importantly, I wanted to pay tribute to the man who became a living symbol of its timeless appeal: Tony Bennett. His career, which spanned over 70 years, is a testament to the enduring power of this art form. From his early hits in the 1950s to his late-career resurgence, including his collaborations with contemporary artists like Lady Gaga, Tony Bennett never wavered in his commitment to the music he loved. He stayed true to the Great American Songbook, to jazz standards, and to the belief that a great song, sung with sincerity, can transcend time.

My connection to Tony Bennett is both personal and profound. I had the honour of meeting him, and while I just missed the chance to sing alongside him, I was able to share a moment with him that I will never forget. Later, after he announced his battle with Alzheimer's, I dedicated a 24-hour singing marathon in his honour, raising funds for the Alzheimer's Society. To my amazement, Tony not only acknowledged my efforts on his social media but personally thanked me, reinforcing the bond I felt with him and his legacy.

This book is not just a historical overview of crooning; it is also a reflection on the profound impact Tony Bennett has had on my life and career as a crooner. It is a tribute to the voices of the past and a look forward to the future of this beautiful art form. As we journey through the origins of crooning, its evolution, and its lasting influence on modern music, I hope to give you a glimpse into the heart of what it means to be a crooner, both then and now.

Music is, at its core, about connection. It's about using one's voice to create something timeless, something that reaches beyond the moment and touches the hearts of listeners across generations. Crooning is the perfect embodiment of that idea, and Tony Bennett was, without a doubt, one of its greatest champions.

I invite you to join me on this journey through the world of crooning, as we honour the past, celebrate the present, and look forward to the future of this timeless tradition.

PROLOGUE

The first time I heard Tony Bennett sing, I was struck by how effortless it all seemed. His voice, warm and inviting, had a way of reaching into the soul, making every note feel personal, every lyric like a shared secret. There was a richness to his sound that transcended the music, it was as if he wasn't just singing to you, but with you, drawing you into a world of memories, emotions, and stories. From that moment, I knew there was something special about Tony Bennett, something timeless.

As I delved deeper into the world of crooning, I realised that this was more than just a style of singing. Crooning was an art form, a way of connecting with people on the deepest level. And Tony Bennett was its master. He embodied everything that made crooning special: the sincerity, the emotional vulnerability, the ability to tell a story with nothing more than the sound of his voice. He didn't need grand gestures or flashy performances, just a microphone, a song, and his heart on his sleeve.

But Tony Bennett's influence didn't end with his music. Over the years, he became a symbol of resilience, grace, and authenticity. He never chased trends or let the passing of time dim his passion for the Great American Songbook. Instead, he stayed true to the songs that mattered to him, performing them with the same love and respect that had defined his career from the start. Whether he was singing to packed concert halls or sharing the stage with contemporary artists, Tony's voice remained a constant, a beacon of timeless artistry in an ever-changing world.

For me, Tony Bennett was more than just an inspiration, he was a personal hero. I had the honour of meeting him, and though I just missed the chance to sing with him in Las Vegas, that brief encounter left an indelible mark on me. Later, when he revealed his battle with Alzheimer's, I felt compelled to do something to honour him. I sang for 24 hours to raise funds for Alzheimer's research, and to my amazement, Tony acknowledged my efforts, highlighting my fundraiser on social media and personally thanking me. That moment, hearing Tony Bennett's words of gratitude, will stay with me for the rest of my life.

This book is my way of paying tribute to Tony Bennett and the world of crooning he helped define. It's a journey through the history of an art form that has touched countless lives and a reflection on how Tony Bennett's voice has become part of the fabric of our collective memories. But more than that, it's a celebration of music's power to connect, to heal, and to endure.

As I share my own story as a crooner, and as we explore the stories of those who came before me, I hope you'll feel the same connection to this timeless tradition that I do. Tony Bennett may no longer be with us, but his voice, his gift to the world, will live on forever. This book is for him, and for the countless people whose lives have been touched by the magic of his music.

Wayne Devlin on Stage

CHAPTER 1: THE BIRTH OF CROONING

When people think of crooning today, they might imagine the smooth, velvety voices of icons like Sinatra, Crosby, or Bennett. But the story of crooning starts long before any of them held a microphone. In fact, crooning as we know it simply wouldn't exist without two key inventions: the microphone and the radio. These technologies, which arrived in the early 20th century, didn't just change the way we listen to music; they fundamentally altered the way singers sang, transforming a public, theatrical art into something intimate and personal. It was the dawn of a new sound.

Before the invention of the microphone, singers had to project their voices to fill vast theatres, halls, and outdoor spaces. It was all about power and range. The style was operatic, demanding volume and clarity so that the furthest audience members could hear every word. But microphones, which became widespread in the 1920s, changed all that. Suddenly, singers didn't need to shout to be heard. They could speak, or sing, softly, and the microphone would carry the nuances of their voice, every breath, every inflection, directly to the audience. The singer could be gentle, even conversational, as though they were singing to each listener personally.

This was the moment when crooning was born. The first true crooners, like Rudy Vallée and Gene Austin, realised that they could use this new technology to bring something new to the art of singing: intimacy. It was no longer about overpowering an orchestra or a noisy room; it was about communicating emotion directly, in a way that felt close and personal. That's why crooning has always been about more than just hitting the right notes. It's about feeling, about creating a connection between the singer and the listener, as though the crooner is speaking to you alone.

With radio also becoming a household fixture in the 1920s, crooning found the perfect medium to flourish. Now, singers could perform live on air and be heard in living rooms across the country, their voices carried through the airwaves to listeners who might never have had the chance to hear them in person. This new connection between singer and listener, fostered by the radio and the microphone, allowed crooners to build enormous, loyal fan bases. People weren't just hearing music; they felt like they were being serenaded in their own homes. The singers who understood this, who learned to use the microphone not as a mere amplification tool but as an extension of their voice, became the first real stars of the crooning era.

Rudy Vallée was one of the earliest crooners to really understand the power of this new style. Known for his soft, almost whispered vocals, he didn't belt out his tunes like the singers before him. Instead, he let the microphone do the work, pulling his audience in with the gentle cadence of his voice. It was almost as if he was inviting you to lean in, to listen more closely. He became a sensation, not because he had the most powerful voice, but because he knew how to use the technology to make his performances feel intimate. And the fans, particularly women, loved it.

Another key figure in the early days was Gene Austin, whose hit "My Blue Heaven" became one of the first million-selling records.

Austin, like Vallée, used the microphone to convey emotion in a subtle, tender way that would have been impossible a decade earlier. It was an entirely new kind of performance. Rather than projecting out to an audience, crooners pulled the audience towards them. They made it feel personal.

The power of this shift cannot be overstated. In a world where most singers were trained to sing as loudly and clearly as possible, the crooners brought a level of intimacy and vulnerability that had never been heard before. They made listeners feel as if they were hearing something private, something meant just for them. And in a way, they were. Crooning became the soundtrack to quiet moments, to romantic evenings, to the kinds of experiences that required a softer touch.

But this new style wasn't without its critics. In fact, some people found crooning downright scandalous. They called it "effeminate" or "too sensual," and some even worried that the close, personal nature of the performances would stir inappropriate feelings in listeners, particularly women. Can you imagine? The idea that a singer's voice, transmitted through the radio into someone's home, could be so intimate that it might create a moral panic. It seems ridiculous now, but in the conservative climate of the 1920s and 1930s, crooning was seen by some as too suggestive, too personal.

Of course, that intimacy was exactly what made crooning so popular. It tapped into something deep and human, an emotional connection that transcended the usual performer-audience dynamic. You weren't just listening to a singer; you were being serenaded. And that's the magic of crooning.

As microphones improved and recording technology became more advanced, the art of crooning evolved too. Singers began to experiment with phrasing, with timing, with the spaces between words. Crooning was never about rushing through a song; it was about lingering on a note, about drawing out the emotion, about letting the listener really feel the sentiment behind the lyrics. That's why so many of the greatest crooners were also the best interpreters of ballads. They knew how to tell a story, not just through the words they sang but through the way they sang them.

It wasn't long before crooning took over the airwaves. From the 1920s through to the 1940s, it became the dominant form of popular singing. Crooners were everywhere, on the radio, in movies, performing in clubs and theatres. The microphone had opened up a whole new world of possibilities, and the best crooners used it to their full advantage.

This new, intimate style of singing was the foundation on which artists like Bing Crosby and Frank Sinatra would build their legendary careers. But before we get to them, it's important to remember those early pioneers, Vallée, Austin, and others, who first realised the power of singing softly, of drawing people in rather than projecting out. Without them, crooning might never have become the art form it is today.

Looking back, it's incredible to think how much of crooning's success comes down to something as simple as a microphone. Without it, none of this would have been possible. But with it, the world of singing, and listening, was changed forever.

CHAPTER 2: BING CROSBY AND THE EARLY PIONEERS

When I think about the defining figure of crooning, the name that always rises to the top of my mind is Bing Crosby. He wasn't just a singer, he was an architect of modern vocal music. If Rudy Vallée and Gene Austin laid the foundation for crooning, Bing Crosby was the one who built it into a cultural phenomenon. His voice, style, and approach to singing not only influenced generations of artists but also shaped the very way people thought about music in the 20th century.

What set Crosby apart from the early pioneers wasn't just his voice, though that alone would have been enough to place him among the greats. It was his ability to understand the power of the microphone and the art of singing softly. Unlike his predecessors, who were still somewhat tied to the old way of performing, projecting their voices as if they were on a stage, Crosby embraced the microphone fully. He realised that, through this new technology, he didn't need to shout or even sing with much force at all. Instead, he could let his voice fall naturally, almost as if he were speaking directly to each listener. He made it feel intimate, as though he were right there in the room with you, whispering secrets through the radio.

Crosby's voice was warm and easy, effortlessly smooth, and endlessly versatile. But more than anything, it was personal. He had an extraordinary ability to convey emotion without overstating it. That was the essence of his crooning style, understated, sincere, and deeply human. He could take a simple phrase and, with just the slightest shift in tone or phrasing, imbue it with a world of meaning. It wasn't about vocal acrobatics or showing off his range, it was about communicating something genuine. That's why so many listeners felt connected to Crosby's music on a personal level. He wasn't just a performer; he was someone they felt they knew.

Crosby's rise to fame came during the 1930s, a time when America, and much of the world, was grappling with the Great Depression. In those tough times, his voice offered something comforting, something familiar, yet somehow new. His recordings and radio broadcasts provided an escape for listeners, and his easy-going style became the soundtrack to an entire generation's experience. It's no wonder he became known as "The Voice of the Century." There was something uniquely reassuring about hearing Crosby sing. It wasn't flashy or brash; it was as though he was telling you, "Everything's going to be alright."

One of the key reasons Crosby was able to connect with his audience so effectively was his background in jazz. He wasn't just a pop singer; he was steeped in jazz, which gave him an incredible sense of rhythm and timing. He knew when to linger on a note, when to pause for effect, and when to let the music carry the emotion. His voice was like an instrument, blending seamlessly with the band rather than standing apart from it. This jazz influence gave Crosby's singing a relaxed, conversational quality that set him apart from the more rigid, formal styles of his contemporaries.

Crosby's partnership with legendary bandleader Paul Whiteman in the early 1930s was a key moment in his career. Whiteman's orchestra was one of the most popular in the country at the time, and his music was a blend of jazz, pop, and classical influences. Singing with Whiteman, Crosby learned how to perform within the context of a larger ensemble while maintaining his own unique voice. His smooth, jazz-inflected style quickly won over audiences, and before long, he was a national sensation.

But it wasn't just radio and live performances that made Crosby a star. He was also a pioneer of recorded music. Crosby understood early on that the microphone wasn't just a tool for live performance; it was also a means of creating a lasting connection with listeners through recordings. In the recording studio, Crosby's voice could be captured with all its subtleties intact. He perfected the art of "close-miking," where the singer would stand close to the microphone, allowing every detail of their voice to be recorded clearly. This technique gave his recordings an intimacy that had never been heard before and changed the way singers approached recording from that point forward.

One of the most iconic examples of Crosby's mastery of this technique is his recording of "White Christmas," a song that would go on to become one of the best-selling singles of all time. Listening to it today, you can still hear the magic in his delivery, the way he softly croons the opening lines, as though he's reminiscing about a memory that's as personal to him as it is to the listener. It's no wonder that the song has endured for so long. Crosby's ability to make each listener feel as though the song is just for them is part of what makes it timeless.

As his fame grew, so did his influence on the music industry. Crosby was more than just a performer, he was a cultural figure whose impact extended far beyond his music. He appeared in films, hosted radio shows, and even became a pioneer of television. But through it all, his singing remained at the heart of everything he did. No matter how many other ventures he pursued, his voice was always his greatest asset. And it was that voice that made him not just a star, but a legend.

Crosby's influence on future generations of singers cannot be overstated. Frank Sinatra, who would later become one of the most iconic crooners in history, often cited Crosby as his greatest influence. In fact, when Sinatra was just starting out, he modelled his singing style after Crosby's, adopting the same smooth, conversational approach that had made Bing famous. But it wasn't just Sinatra, Crosby's fingerprints can be found in the work of countless singers who followed in his footsteps. From Tony Bennett to Dean Martin, from Perry Como to even modern-day crooners like Michael Bublé, Bing Crosby's legacy is woven into the fabric of popular music.

But what really makes Crosby's contribution to crooning so profound isn't just his technical skill or his influence on other artists. It's the fact that he made crooning feel personal. He turned singing into something intimate, something that spoke directly to the listener's heart. In a world that often feels noisy and chaotic, that's a gift. Crosby didn't just sing songs, he shared a part of himself with his audience, and that's what makes his music endure.

As a crooner myself, I often think about what it means to sing in the tradition of Bing Crosby. To me, it's about more than just hitting the notes or mastering a certain vocal technique. It's about creating a connection, about making the listener feel something. That's what Crosby did, and that's what I aim to do every time I step up to the microphone. Crooning, at its best, is an art form that touches the soul. And no one understood that better than Bing Crosby.

CHAPTER 3: FRANK SINATRA AND THE CROONER AS A CULTURAL ICON

If Bing Crosby laid the groundwork for crooning, then Frank Sinatra elevated it to a level that no one could have predicted. Sinatra wasn't just a singer, he was the embodiment of a cultural movement. He took the intimacy of crooning and added something new: swagger. He turned the crooner from a gentle, romantic figure into a global icon of style, confidence, and raw emotion. Where Crosby had been warm and reassuring, Sinatra was cool and self-assured, yet vulnerable in a way that resonated deeply with audiences around the world. In Sinatra's hands, crooning became more than just a style of singing, it became an expression of life itself.

My own journey as a crooner has been shaped by Sinatra in ways that are hard to fully explain. His music, his presence, his whole attitude towards singing, it was magnetic. And not just for me. For countless singers who came after him, Frank Sinatra was the standard. He was the crooner who turned a style into a lifestyle, making it cool to be vulnerable, to express deep emotions, while still maintaining that tough, untouchable exterior. Sinatra knew how to walk that fine line between being the guy every man wanted to be and the one every woman wanted to be with. It was his ability to balance those elements that made him such an extraordinary performer and such an enduring figure.

What made Sinatra's crooning stand out wasn't just his voice, though of course, his voice was extraordinary. He had this incredible ability to shape a song, to bend it to his will, and make it entirely his own. He wasn't simply singing notes; he was telling a story. Every lyric, every phrase was carefully considered, delivered with precision and emotion. He had a way of phrasing that felt so effortless, but you knew every line had been meticulously crafted to hit just the right note with the audience.

Sinatra's journey to becoming the ultimate crooner icon wasn't an easy one. He started out in the big band era, singing with groups like the Harry James Orchestra and later, the Tommy Dorsey Orchestra. It was during his time with Dorsey that Sinatra began to refine his craft, learning the intricacies of phrasing and breath control. Dorsey was known for his smooth trombone playing, and Sinatra would later credit him with teaching him how to "play" his voice like an instrument. He learned to sustain notes, to control his breath, and to use the spaces between phrases as much as the phrases themselves. It was this training that would later define Sinatra's signature style.

In those early years, Sinatra was already a star, especially with the bobby-soxers, those teenage girls who would scream and faint at the sight of him. But it wasn't until he went solo in the 1940s that he truly became the cultural force we know today. Sinatra's early solo career was marked by a series of ups and downs. He had enormous success in the mid-1940s, but by the early 1950s, his career had hit a rough patch. He'd lost his voice temporarily, and his record sales had started to decline. For a while, it seemed like his time in the spotlight might be over.

But if there's one thing Sinatra was known for, it was his ability to bounce back. In 1953, he made a dramatic comeback, both in film and in music. His role in the film From Here to Eternity won him an Academy Award, and it revitalised his career. Around the same time, he signed with Capitol Records, where he began working with arrangers like Nelson Riddle. This partnership would prove to be one of the most important of his career. Riddle's lush, orchestral arrangements perfectly complemented Sinatra's voice, allowing him to explore a deeper, more mature sound.

It was during this period that Sinatra recorded some of his most iconic albums, including In the Wee Small Hours and Songs for Swingin' Lovers!. These records were unlike anything else at the time. They were concept albums, designed to be listened to from start to finish, with each song telling part of a larger emotional journey. Sinatra's voice on these albums was rich, expressive, and heartbreakingly human. He wasn't just crooning anymore, he was baring his soul.

One of the things that always struck me about Sinatra's singing was his ability to convey both strength and vulnerability. He could sing a love song and make you feel the weight of every word, as though he were speaking directly to you. But at the same time, there was always a sense of resilience, of defiance. Even when he sang about heartbreak, there was this undercurrent of strength, as if he were saying, "Yes, love hurts, but I'll survive." That balance between emotion and control is what made Sinatra so compelling, and it's something I've tried to emulate in my own singing.

Sinatra was also a master of reinvention. Throughout his career, he adapted to changing musical trends while always staying true to his core identity as a crooner. In the 1960s, when rock and roll was taking over, Sinatra released Strangers in the Night, a song that became one of his biggest hits. He could have easily been overshadowed by the rise of bands like The Beatles, but instead, he found a way to remain relevant by embracing the changes while still maintaining his unique style. His ability to evolve with the times without losing what made him special is one of the reasons why his music still resonates with audiences today.

But it wasn't just Sinatra's music that made him a cultural icon, it was his whole persona. He embodied the ideal of the cool, confident, self-made man. He wasn't just a crooner; he was a symbol of success, of living life on your own terms. The Rat Pack era only solidified this image. Sinatra, along with Dean Martin, Sammy Davis Jr., and the rest of the gang, became synonymous with a certain kind of glamorous, hard-living, but always-in-control lifestyle. They were the kings of Las Vegas, the ultimate showmen, and their larger-than-life personalities became as much a part of their appeal as their music.

Sinatra's influence on the world of crooning, and on music in general, can't be overstated. He took a style that was already popular and elevated it to new heights, both musically and culturally. His phrasing, his emotion, his ability to connect with an audience, these are the things that made Sinatra more than just a singer. He was an artist. And as a fellow crooner, I've spent years studying his work, trying to understand how he was able to capture that magic time and time again.

Sinatra's legacy is everywhere. It's in the way we think about crooning today, in the way modern artists approach singing with a sense of storytelling and emotional depth. But perhaps more importantly, it's in the way he taught us that singing isn't just about technique or hitting the right notes. It's about connecting with people, about sharing something real. And that, to me, is what crooning is all about.

CHAPTER 4: THE GOLDEN AGE OF RADIO AND TELEVISION

The rise of crooning wasn't just about the singers themselves; it was also about the new technology that brought their voices into people's homes. Radio and television didn't just give crooners a platform, they changed the very way music was consumed and experienced. The golden age of crooning was inseparable from the golden age of radio and television, as these mediums allowed singers to develop intimate relationships with their audiences in a way that had never been possible before.

In the early 20th century, before radio became a common fixture in households, music was something people mostly experienced live. If you wanted to hear a singer, you'd have to go to a concert, a theatre, or perhaps a dance hall. The intimacy that crooners like Rudy Vallée, Bing Crosby, and later Frank Sinatra developed wouldn't have been possible without the invention of radio, which turned listening into a shared but deeply personal experience.

As radios became more affordable and widespread in the 1920s and 1930s, crooning naturally found its home on the airwaves. The intimacy of the crooning style was a perfect match for radio, where a voice that sounded as though it was meant for you alone could captivate listeners in their living rooms, kitchens, and bedrooms. Radio erased the physical distance between performer and audience, and crooning, already a style built on emotional closeness, flourished in this new medium. For the first time, singers didn't need to project their voices to the back of a theatre. They could sing softly, allowing every nuance and breath to be heard as though they were sitting right next to you. And listeners responded in kind. The emotional connection that crooning fostered was strengthened by the personal nature of radio listening. You weren't just hearing a song, you were being sung to.

This was something that I've always found fascinating about crooning. It was a style perfectly suited to the technology of the time. Crooners like Bing Crosby, with his easy-going, conversational style, or even someone like Frank Sinatra, who could turn a phrase with such precision, understood that the microphone wasn't just an amplification tool, it was an extension of their voice. The microphone allowed them to create an experience that felt personal and intimate. And with radio, this experience could be shared by millions of people at once.

The power of radio during this time can't be understated. Not only did it bring crooners into homes across the country, but it also shaped the careers of these singers in unprecedented ways. Bing Crosby, for example, became a household name largely due to his regular radio broadcasts. His show, The Kraft Music Hall, ran for nearly a decade, and during that time, Crosby's voice became as familiar to Americans as their own family's. People tuned in every week not just to hear the music, but to be part of something that felt personal and immediate.

Crosby's radio success wasn't unique, though. Many of the great crooners of the era had their own radio shows, which helped them build lasting relationships with their audiences. Radio wasn't just a platform for promoting records, it was a place where listeners could develop a real connection with the performers. It's no surprise that these shows were incredibly popular, especially during the tough years of the Great Depression and World War II. People needed an escape, and crooners provided it. Their soothing, romantic voices were a balm during those difficult times, offering a sense of hope, comfort, and familiarity.

I often think about how radio must have felt during those days, sitting at home with your family, listening to Bing Crosby or Frank Sinatra sing just for you. The world outside may have been chaotic, but in those moments, you could lose yourself in the music, in the warmth of a voice that seemed to speak directly to your soul. That's what crooning did, it created a bridge between the performer and the listener, closing the distance between them in a way that no other style of singing had before.

And just as radio was crucial to the rise of crooning, so too was television. As television sets began to enter homes in the late 1940s and 1950s, crooners quickly adapted to this new medium. They weren't just voices anymore, they were faces, personalities, larger-than-life figures who could now be seen as well as heard. Shows like The Ed Sullivan Show and The Colgate Comedy Hour brought crooners into living rooms across the country, giving audiences the chance to see their favourite singers perform live on screen.

This shift to television was important for a number of reasons. First, it helped crooners become even more iconic. People had spent years listening to voices like Sinatra's on the radio, but now they could see the man behind the music, the way he moved, the way he carried himself, the emotions on his face as he sang. Sinatra, with his cool, charismatic stage presence, was a natural fit for television. He didn't just sing a song; he performed it, and the visual element added a whole new layer to his appeal.

But television also added pressure. With radio, crooners could rely solely on their voices to carry the emotion of a song. With television, they had to be fully realised performers, able to connect with audiences both sonically and visually. The most successful crooners of this era, Sinatra, Dean Martin, Nat King Cole, were able to do just that. They weren't just great singers; they were entertainers in every sense of the word.

Dean Martin, for instance, was the ultimate showman. His relaxed, seemingly effortless performances were perfect for television. He could make you feel like you were sitting in a club with him, enjoying a drink, as he crooned through a ballad or swung through a jazzy number. And Martin wasn't alone. Tony Bennett, another crooner who thrived in the television era, brought a level of emotional depth and sincerity to his performances that made him a favourite with TV audiences.

But if there was one crooner who truly capitalised on the power of television, it was Nat King Cole. Cole was not only a brilliant singer and pianist but also one of the first African American artists to host his own national television show, The Nat King Cole Show. It was a groundbreaking moment, not just for Cole but for television itself. He brought crooning to a whole new audience and became a trailblazer in the fight for racial equality in the entertainment industry. His smooth, velvety voice and dignified stage presence made him a beloved figure across the country, and his influence on crooning is still felt today.

Television may have added a visual element to crooning, but at its heart, the essence of the style remained the same. It was about creating a connection, about making the listener (or viewer, in this case) feel something personal and real. Crooners understood that, whether they were performing for a live audience, singing on the radio, or appearing on television, their job was to reach out and touch the hearts of their audience. They did this not with grand gestures or loud proclamations, but with the quiet power of a voice that spoke directly to the listener's emotions.

As a modern crooner, I often reflect on what it must have been like to perform during this golden age of radio and television. These platforms helped turn crooning into a cultural phenomenon, and they gave singers the chance to connect with audiences in ways that had never been possible before. Even today, as I step up to the microphone, I think about the power of that connection. Whether I'm performing live, recording in the studio, or sharing my music online, my goal is always the same, to make the listener feel like I'm singing just for them.

CHAPTER 5: TONY BENNETT'S JOURNEY

There are few names in the world of crooning that resonate as deeply as Tony Bennett's. His voice, rich with emotion and authenticity, spans decades of music history. Bennett isn't just a crooner, he's a living testament to the timelessness of the art form, a bridge between generations of listeners who've found solace, joy, and inspiration in his songs. His journey as an artist has been nothing short of remarkable, and for me, as a fellow crooner, his influence looms large.

Tony Bennett's rise to stardom is a story rooted in perseverance, talent, and a deep love for music. Born Anthony Dominick Benedetto in 1926 in Astoria, Queens, New York, Bennett grew up in a working-class Italian-American family during the Great Depression. From a young age, he was exposed to the arts, with his father a fan of opera and his uncle a tap dancer. But it was after his service in World War II that Bennett's musical journey really began. When he returned from the war, he pursued singing professionally, studying under the G.I. Bill and performing in clubs around New York. His big break came when he was discovered by Pearl Bailey and introduced to Bob Hope, who suggested the name change from Benedetto to Bennett, a name that would soon become legendary.

What sets Bennett apart from other crooners of his time is his remarkable versatility and longevity. His career, which began in the late 1940s, has endured well into the 21st century. He's outlasted nearly all of his peers, not by chasing trends or adapting to the changing musical landscape, but by staying true to his core: that smooth, expressive voice and his deep connection to the American songbook.

Bennett first found success in the 1950s with hits like Because of You and Rags to Riches, songs that showcased his incredible range and ability to convey raw emotion. But it was his 1962 recording of I Left My Heart in San Francisco that truly cemented his place in music history. That song, with its poignant lyrics and Bennett's flawless delivery, became an anthem not just for the city of San Francisco, but for all those who've ever felt a longing for home, or for a place of belonging. It's a song that has followed Bennett throughout his career, and no matter how many times I've heard it, it never loses its emotional impact.

What I've always admired about Tony Bennett is his unwavering dedication to his craft. He's never been about flash or gimmicks. While many artists reinvented themselves over the decades, chasing new trends, Bennett remained true to his love of jazz, the Great American Songbook, and traditional pop. He wasn't interested in following the latest fads; instead, he focused on perfecting his art. His collaborations with great jazz musicians like Count Basie, Stan Getz, and Bill Evans are a testament to his deep respect for the music and the musicians who create it. In a way, Bennett's career has been a masterclass in how to sustain artistic integrity while still evolving as a performer.

Thanks to my wife, Val, who arranged it, I had the incredible fortune of meeting Tony Bennett later in his life, and though I just missed the opportunity to sing with him in Las Vegas at the Flamingo Casino, I did have the honour of meeting him at the Bridgewater Hall in Manchester. I'll never forget that moment.

Meeting one of your idols is always a humbling experience, and Bennett was everything I imagined he would be, gracious, warm, and down-to-earth. It was a brief meeting, but it left a lasting impression on me. I had spent years studying his music, learning from his phrasing, his timing, his ability to hold an audience in the palm of his hand. To finally meet the man behind the voice was an incredible privilege.

But my connection to Tony Bennett runs deeper than just that meeting. In 2021, when Tony announced that he was living with Alzheimer's disease, it hit me hard. Here was this man, this legend, who had given so much to the world through his music, facing such a cruel and debilitating illness. It felt personal to me, and I knew I wanted to do something to honour him.

So, I did what I knew best, I sang. In Tony's honour, I embarked on a 24-hour non-stop singing marathon to raise funds for the Alzheimer's Society. It was one of the most challenging things I've ever done, both physically and emotionally. Singing for 24 hours straight is no easy task, but I wasn't doing it for me. I was doing it for Tony and for everyone affected by Alzheimer's. As a crooner, I've always believed in the power of music to heal, to bring people together, and to honour those we care about. This was my way of paying tribute to a man who had inspired me throughout my career.

The response to my fundraiser was overwhelming, but the moment that meant the most to me was when Tony Bennett himself acknowledged my efforts. Tony's team highlighted my fundraising on his social media, spreading the word to his vast audience. And then, the personal note came. Tony Bennett wrote to me, thanking me for what I had done in his honour. I still have that letter, it's something I'll treasure for the rest of my life. There was a moment of deep connection in that exchange, as if the years I had spent admiring and learning from Tony had come full circle.

I'll never forget the phone call I received from Tony. Speaking to him on the phone, hearing him thank me personally, was a surreal and emotional experience. Here I was, a crooner from Manchester, being thanked by one of the greatest voices of all time. That phone call reminded me of the power of music to connect us, across generations, across miles, even in the face of adversity. Tony Bennett had always been my musical hero, but in that moment, he became something more, a mentor, a friend.

Tony Bennett's influence on me, and on the world of crooning, is immeasurable. His ability to blend jazz with traditional pop, to maintain both technical precision and deep emotional sincerity, is something I strive for every time I step up to the microphone. He's shown us all that crooning isn't just about the notes or the songs, it's about creating a bond with the audience, about telling a story through music, and about being true to yourself as an artist. In a world that's constantly changing, Tony Bennett has remained a steady presence, reminding us that some things, like a beautiful song, sung from the heart, are timeless.

As I continue my own journey as a crooner, I often think about Tony Bennett and the lessons he's taught me, both through his music and through the brief, but meaningful, connection we shared. Crooning isn't just a style of singing, it's a way of life. It's about sincerity, about honesty, about creating something that resonates on a deep emotional level. That's what Tony Bennett has done for decades, and that's what I aim to do every time I perform.

CHAPTER 6: MY STORY BEGINS: DISCOVERING CROONING

My first memory of crooning is almost as vivid today as it was when I experienced it all those years ago. The smooth, velvety sound of a voice coming through the speakers, filling the room with warmth and emotion, it was like nothing I'd ever heard before. I was hooked. That sound, the intimacy, the connection, the simplicity, was what I wanted to create. In that moment, I knew that crooning would become more than just music to me; it would become a way of life.

Growing up, I wasn't exactly surrounded by music. I wasn't born into a family of musicians or raised in a home where jazz standards were played on repeat. My love for crooning came from a different place, from an appreciation for storytelling, for the kind of voice that could make you stop in your tracks and really feel something. I always admired the way these singers could take a song and make it their own, turning it into an experience, a moment shared between them and the listener.

In those early days, it was the voices of the legends that captivated me on my fathers record collection, Bing Crosby, Nat King Cole, Perry Como, Frank Sinatra, Dean Martin, Matt Monro and, of course, Tony Bennett. They had something special. It wasn't just their technical ability or the beauty of their voices, though that was certainly part of it. It was the way they connected with the audience. Crooning isn't about belting out a tune or showing off your range. It's about subtlety, about drawing people in and making them feel like you're singing just for them. That's what made crooning different from any other style of singing, and that's what drew me to it.

The first time I really tried my hand at crooning was in front of a small crowd of parents and pupils at my junior school, Woodhouse Primary where I sang 'Leaning on a Lampost' at a school play. I didnt sing again publicly until I got up on stage one night at a local pub. I can still remember the nerves, the feeling that I wasn't sure if I'd be able to pull it off, to deliver the song in a way that felt genuine and true to the tradition of crooning. But as soon as I started singing, something clicked. It was as if all those years of listening to the greats had somehow seeped into me. I wasn't trying to imitate them, but their influence was unmistakable. I was finding my own voice within that tradition, learning how to express myself through the music that had meant so much to me growing up.

I've always believed that crooning is about telling a story, and in that moment, standing in front of that small audience, I felt like I was sharing something real, something meaningful. The response was encouraging, people seemed to feel what I was trying to convey. That's the beauty of crooning; it's not about impressing people with flashy vocal tricks or complicated melodies. It's about making them feel something, about creating a connection.

As I continued to perform, my love for the art of crooning only deepened. I found myself drawn to the songs that told a story, the ones that allowed me to express emotion in a subtle, nuanced way. The Great American Songbook became my musical bible, songs by Gershwin, Porter, Berlin, and Rodgers and Hart. These were the tunes that resonated with me, the ones that seemed timeless.

Singing them felt like stepping into history, like carrying on a tradition that had been passed down through generations.

It wasn't just about the music, though. Crooning, for me, has always been as much about the style, the presence, the way you carry yourself as an artist. There's an elegance to crooning, a kind of understated charm that sets it apart from other forms of performance. It's about creating an atmosphere, about taking the audience on a journey with you, whether you're singing a joyful, swinging tune or a melancholy ballad. And it's about respect, respect for the music, for the audience, and for the tradition.

I soon realised that crooning wasn't just a style of singing, it was a way of connecting with people. And that connection is what has always driven me. Whether I'm performing in front of a packed theatre or a small group in a club, my goal is always the same: to create a moment, a shared experience that brings people together through music. That's the magic of crooning, it has the ability to make people feel something deeply, to remind them of memories, of love, of loss, of hope. There's a timelessness to it that transcends trends and fads.

As I began to perform more regularly, I started to carve out my own path as a crooner. I wasn't trying to be the next Sinatra or Crosby, those were impossible shoes to fill. But I wanted to bring my own voice to the tradition, to honour the greats while still being true to who I was as an artist. It was a delicate balance, and one that I'm still learning every day. But that's the beauty of being a crooner, it's a lifelong journey, a constant evolution as you refine your craft and discover new ways to connect with your audience.

For me, crooning has always been about more than just singing. It's about telling a story, about expressing emotion in a way that feels real and genuine. When I'm on stage, I'm not just performing a song, I'm sharing a piece of myself with the audience. And in return, I'm asking them to share a piece of themselves with me. It's a two-way street, a relationship built on trust and mutual understanding. That's what makes crooning so special, it's personal, intimate, and deeply human.

As I look back on my journey so far, I'm filled with gratitude for the opportunities I've had to share this incredible art form with others. Crooning has taken me to places I never could have imagined, from small pubs in Manchester to some of the most iconic stages in the world. But no matter where I'm performing, the goal is always the same: to make people feel something, to create a moment of connection that transcends the everyday and speaks to something deeper.

That's what crooning has always been about for me, and that's why I continue to do it, day after day, year after year. It's not about fame or recognition, it's about the music, the stories, and the connection with the audience. That's what keeps me going, and that's what makes this journey so incredibly rewarding.

CHAPTER 7: THE LAS VEGAS DREAM: A NEAR CHANCE WITH TONY BENNETT

There's something magical about Las Vegas, a place where dreams seem tantalisingly within reach, where the very air hums with possibility. For a crooner like me, the idea of performing in Vegas holds a certain allure. After all, this is the city where legends like Frank Sinatra, Dean Martin, and, of course, Tony Bennett made their mark. So, when I found myself in Las Vegas with the possibility to sing alongside Tony Bennett, it felt like the stars had aligned. But, as fate would have it, life had other plans, and that dream would remain just out of reach.

The Flamingo Casino is one of those iconic venues that echoes with the history of crooning. It's a place where voices like Sinatra's once filled the room, where the classic showmanship of the Rat Pack era lives on. Being in a city that was synonymous with crooning felt like a full-circle moment for me. Vegas is, after all, the spiritual home of this kind of music, a place where crooners thrive, where their intimate style of singing perfectly complements the glamour and excitement of the city. To be there, breathing in that air, was already a dream come true.

The opportunity to sing with Tony Bennett arose almost by chance. I was set to perform as a warm up act at the Flamingo, and Tony had been invited along to the event. It wasn't just any show, this was for Wayne Newton, and Tony, one of the greatest crooners of all time, a man whose voice had shaped the very landscape of popular music for decades, was going to be there on one of the evenings as a special guest. The thought of sharing the stage with him, even for a moment, was enough to set my heart racing. To be on the same stage as someone whose career had been an endless source of inspiration for me was almost too good to be true.

I had been performing for years at this point, honing my craft and finding my own voice within the tradition of crooning. But to sing with Tony Bennett? That was something else entirely. The mere thought of standing next to him, microphone in hand, was enough to make me feel like a wide-eyed kid again, dreaming of the impossible. For me, this wasn't just about singing a song. It was about connecting with someone who had helped shape the way I viewed music, someone whose influence had been so deeply ingrained in my own journey as a crooner.

The day he arrived at the Casino, I could feel the excitement in the building as he walked in. I had been told that there was a possibility, just a possibility, that I might get the chance to sing with Tony. Nothing was set in stone, but the idea that it could happen was enough to send my mind racing. I rehearsed in my head, imagining what it would be like, picturing the moment when our voices would blend together in harmony. I could see it so clearly: Tony's smooth, seasoned voice carrying the melody, while I followed his lead, adding my own touch to the performance. It was a dream scenario, and I allowed myself to believe that it might actually happen.

But, as life often goes, the moment slipped away before it could fully take shape. The opportunity to sing with Tony Bennett, the one I had dreamed of, vanished just as quickly as it had appeared. Maybe it was the schedule, maybe it was logistics, or maybe it was just one of those twists of fate that we can't control. Whatever the reason, it wasn't meant to be. I finished my set and had to leave to go to another gig at the Golden Nugget Casino, and it was then, moments after I left, that Tony took to the stage and performed with another singer, I could imagine his voice as powerful and emotive as ever, filling the room with the kind of magic that only he can create. And though I wasn't standing next to him, I'm glad that another young crooner had that once in a lifetime experience.

There's a strange kind of bittersweetness in those near-miss moments. Part of me was disappointed, of course, because the chance to sing with Tony Bennett was something I had dreamed of for years. But at the same time, there was something beautiful in just being close to that moment, in being part of the experience. Whenever I watched Tony perform after that day, knowing that I had almost shared the stage with him, was surreal. It was a reminder that, even when things don't work out exactly as we hope, we're still part of something bigger, still connected to the music and the moments that shape our lives.

I may not have sung with Tony Bennett that night in Las Vegas, but the experience left a lasting impression on me. Being so close to someone who had been such a major influence on my career made me realise just how far I had come. I had spent years listening to Tony's records, learning from his phrasing, his timing, his effortless ability to make a song feel both grand and intimate at the same time. And here I was, not just as a fan, but as a fellow crooner, standing on the edge of a dream that almost came true.

What struck me most about Tony whenever I watched him perform, was his humility. Despite being a living legend, despite having a career that spanned decades, he carried himself with such grace, such generosity. There was no ego, no sense of superiority, just a deep love for the music and for the people he was singing to. That, to me, is the essence of crooning. It's not about the fame or the accolades, though Tony certainly had plenty of both. It's about the connection, the ability to reach out through the music and touch people's hearts. That's what Tony has always done, and it's what I strive to do in my own performances.

In a way, missing the chance to sing with Tony Bennett was a lesson in itself. It reminded me that the journey is just as important as the destination, that sometimes the moments we don't get are just as meaningful as the ones we do. I left Las Vegas with a renewed sense of purpose, inspired by Tony's performance and by the realisation that, while I may not have shared the stage with him that night, I was still part of something special. I was carrying on a tradition that Tony had helped shape, and that was enough for me.

The experience also deepened my appreciation for the unpredictability of life as a performer. Sometimes, things don't go the way we plan. We miss opportunities, we face disappointments, but we keep going because the music, the act of singing, of sharing a moment with an audience, is worth it. And in those moments, when I'm up on stage, crooning my heart out, I often think back to that night in Las Vegas and the dream that almost came true. It's a reminder that every performance, every opportunity, is part of a bigger journey, one that's filled with highs and lows, near-misses and triumphs.

Though I didn't get to sing with Tony Bennett that night, my connection to him would grow in ways I never could have anticipated. That near miss in Las Vegas was just the beginning of a relationship with Tony that would come to mean more to me than I ever imagined. But that's a story for another chapter.

CHAPTER 8: THE GLOBAL IMPACT OF CROONING

C rooning may have found its roots in the United States, but the beauty of the style, its intimacy, its emotional depth, knew no borders. As radio waves and records carried the voices of Bing Crosby, Frank Sinatra, and Tony Bennett across oceans, crooning slowly but surely made its way into homes, clubs, and concert halls around the world. From London to Paris, from Tokyo to Buenos Aires, crooning became a truly global phenomenon.

What is it about crooning that transcends language and culture? That's a question I've asked myself many times, especially when I've found myself performing for audiences far from home. Part of it, I think, is the universal appeal of the voice. A well-sung melody can bypass the barriers of language, speaking directly to the heart in a way that's immediate and personal. Crooners understood this intuitively. They didn't need to shout or dazzle with vocal gymnastics; instead, they pulled the listener in with a softer, more direct approach. It was as if they were speaking to you, not at you, and that kind of connection isn't bound by geography or culture.

The American crooners of the 20th century became global

ambassadors for this intimate style of singing. As their records were pressed and distributed worldwide, they found new audiences who, though separated by language and culture, recognised the emotional honesty of crooning. Bing Crosby, with his easy-going, conversational tone, became a household name not just in America, but across Europe and beyond. His Christmas classic, White Christmas, is still sung all over the world, no matter what language people speak.

And then there was Frank Sinatra, whose music found an enthusiastic audience far beyond the United States. His crooning wasn't just about love songs, it was about life, about the ups and downs we all go through. Sinatra's voice, full of swagger but also vulnerability, spoke to something universal, and it wasn't long before he became an international star. In the UK, in particular, Sinatra's influence was undeniable. His records flew off the shelves, and his visits to London were greeted with fanfare that rivalled that of the Beatles in their early days.

As a British crooner myself, I've always been fascinated by how deeply this American-born art form resonated in the UK. There's something about the British sensibility, our love of romance, our appreciation for understated elegance, that made crooning feel like a natural fit. During the post-war years, British audiences fell in love with the American crooners, but it didn't stop there. Soon enough, homegrown crooners began to emerge, putting their own spin on the style and carrying on the tradition in their own way.

One of the most notable British crooners to rise to fame was Matt Monro. Often referred to as "The Man with the Golden Voice," Monro brought a distinctly British charm to the art of crooning. His voice was smooth and effortless, his phrasing impeccable. In many ways, Monro embodied what made crooning so special, he wasn't flashy or dramatic, but there was a sincerity in his voice that drew people in. His hits, like Born Free and From Russia with Love, became classics not just in the UK, but around the world. Monro proved that crooning wasn't just an American phenomenon, it was a style that could be embraced by anyone, anywhere.

Monro wasn't alone. Other British crooners like Engelbert Humperdinck followed in his footsteps, each bringing their own unique flavour to the tradition. What's interesting to me is how these British crooners managed to stay true to the essence of the style while also infusing it with something distinctly British. There's a subtlety to British crooning, a kind of quiet restraint that feels different from the American approach. But at its core, it's all about the same thing: connecting with the listener on a deep, emotional level.

Europe, in general, has had a long love affair with crooning. French crooners like Charles Trenet and later, Charles Aznavour, brought a certain romanticism to the style that felt distinctly French but still in keeping with the crooning tradition. In France, crooning wasn't just about the American songbook, it was about chanson, about telling stories of love, loss, and life's bittersweet moments. Aznavour, in particular, became a legend in his own right, a singer whose voice carried the weight of his experiences, yet always felt intimate and personal. He was often referred to as the "French Sinatra," and it's easy to see why. His ability to tell a story through song, to make the listener feel every emotion, was the hallmark of a true crooner.

In Latin America, crooning took on a different, but no less powerful, form. Artists like Julio Iglesias and Luis Miguel brought a passionate, soulful approach to crooning that resonated with audiences across the Spanish-speaking world. Julio Iglesias, with his smooth, romantic voice, became one of the best-selling artists of all time, his records selling millions across Europe and Latin America. Luis Miguel, who followed in Iglesias' footsteps, kept the tradition alive with his powerful interpretations of boleros, songs that, much like the classic American standards, told stories of love and longing. These Latin crooners brought a sense of drama and intensity to the style, but at its core, it was still about that intimate connection between singer and listener.

And then, of course, there's Japan, where crooning found a particularly devoted audience. Japanese crooners like Frank Nagai and Yukio Hashi brought the style to a new culture, blending traditional Japanese musical elements with the American crooning sound. What's fascinating about crooning in Japan is how seamlessly it was adapted to fit the cultural context. The themes of love, longing, and heartache, so central to crooning, resonated deeply with Japanese audiences, and crooners became beloved figures in the Japanese music scene.

As crooning spread around the world, it became clear that this wasn't just a passing trend, it was a universal language of emotion. No matter where you were from, no matter what language you spoke, there was something about a crooner's voice that could reach across the divides of culture and geography. And that, I think, is what makes crooning so timeless.

I've been fortunate enough in my own career to perform for audiences far beyond the UK. From small clubs in Europe to international venues, I've seen firsthand how deeply people connect with crooning, no matter where they're from. There's something about this music that cuts through the noise, something that speaks to the shared experiences we all have, love, loss, joy, sorrow. When I'm on stage, whether in Manchester or New York, I feel that connection with the audience, that sense that we're all in this moment together, sharing something real and true.

The global impact of crooning is a testament to the power of the human voice, to its ability to transcend borders and bring people together. It's a reminder that, no matter where we come from, we all have the capacity to feel deeply, to be moved by a beautiful melody and a heartfelt lyric. That's what crooning has always been about, creating a connection that goes beyond words, beyond culture, and straight to the heart.

As a crooner, I feel incredibly fortunate to be part of this global tradition. It's humbling to think about the generations of singers who've come before me, each bringing their own voice to this timeless art form, and about the audiences who've found something meaningful in the music. Crooning is more than just a style of singing, it's a way of connecting with the world, one song at a time.

CHAPTER 9: NAT KING COLE AND THE ART OF SMOOTH SINGING

If ever there was a voice that seemed to glide effortlessly over every note, it was Nat King Cole's. His smooth, soothing tones made him one of the most iconic crooners of all time, and his music continues to resonate with audiences around the world even today. What Cole brought to crooning wasn't just a mastery of vocal technique; it was a rare ability to make every song feel intimate, warm, and personal. His voice wasn't just an instrument, it was a presence, a companion that seemed to understand your joys, your sorrows, your hopes, and your dreams.

Nat King Cole's journey as a crooner was somewhat unique. Unlike many of the crooners who started out as pure vocalists, Cole was first and foremost a jazz pianist. His early career was rooted in the world of jazz, leading his trio and gaining recognition for his skill at the piano. But it wasn't long before the world would discover that his voice was just as extraordinary as his piano playing. In fact, Cole's voice would go on to eclipse his reputation as a pianist, though he continued to play and integrate his piano work into his performances throughout his career.

What always struck me about Nat King Cole was the incredible effortlessness of his voice. He made it sound easy, as though singing were as natural as breathing. Every note he sang seemed to flow from him with a kind of graceful precision that few singers could ever hope to match. And yet, there was nothing cold or clinical about Cole's delivery. His voice was full of warmth, full of emotion, but always in control. Listening to Cole sing is like being wrapped in a soft, comforting blanket, there's a sense of calm, of peace, that washes over you with each song.

Cole's ability to convey emotion with such subtlety is part of what makes him a true master of crooning. He didn't need to belt out a song or rely on vocal acrobatics to make his point. Instead, he let the nuances of his voice do the work. A slight change in phrasing, a soft inflection, a gentle pause, all of these elements were carefully crafted to draw the listener in, to make them feel as though the song was meant for them alone.

One of the best examples of this is Cole's rendition of Mona Lisa. The song, which became one of his most enduring hits, is a perfect showcase for his understated style. The way Cole eases into the melody, letting each word roll off his tongue with a quiet elegance, creates a sense of intimacy that's hard to describe. It's as if he's singing just for you, sharing a secret, inviting you into a world where love and beauty reign supreme. There's no need for grand gestures or dramatic flourishes, Cole's voice says it all with quiet grace.

But Cole wasn't just a master of ballads. He could swing with the best of them, bringing his jazz background into his crooning in a way that felt effortless and natural. Songs like Straighten Up and Fly Right and Route 66 showed off his ability to navigate more upbeat, swinging tunes without losing any of that smooth, easy-going charm. Even when the tempo picked up, Cole's voice remained as relaxed and in control as ever, gliding through the music with a sense of ease that belied the complexity of what he was doing.

Nat King Cole was also a trailblazer in more ways than one. As one of the first African American artists to achieve mainstream success in the predominantly white world of pop music, Cole broke down barriers that had kept so many talented Black artists from reaching wider audiences. His success wasn't just about his talent, it was about his determination to be seen and heard as a musician first and foremost, regardless of the colour of his skin. In a time when segregation and racism were rampant in America, Cole's music transcended those divisions, reaching people of all races and backgrounds.

In 1956, Nat King Cole made history by becoming the first African American to host a national television show, The Nat King Cole Show. It was a groundbreaking moment, not just for Cole, but for American television. Here was a Black man, hosting his own show, performing for a national audience, and being celebrated for his music. It was a major step forward for racial equality in the entertainment industry, though the road wasn't always easy for Cole. The show struggled to find national sponsors, as many companies were reluctant to advertise on a programme hosted by a Black man. Despite this, Cole remained gracious and professional, never allowing the challenges he faced to diminish the power of his music or his commitment to his craft.

One of the things I've always admired about Nat King Cole is the way he carried himself through all of this. He never seemed to let the racism and prejudice he encountered weigh him down. Instead, he rose above it, letting his music speak for itself. His voice became a beacon of hope and dignity, not just for African American audiences, but for anyone who believed in the power of music to bring people together.

And that's exactly what Nat King Cole did, he brought people together. His music, whether it was a tender ballad or a swinging jazz number, had a way of transcending divisions and creating a sense of unity among listeners. It didn't matter where you came from or what your background was, when you listened to Nat King Cole, you were part of something bigger, something that went beyond race, class, or nationality. You were part of a shared experience, a moment of beauty and emotion that only music can create.

As a crooner myself, I've spent countless hours studying Nat King Cole's recordings, trying to understand what made his voice so special. It's not something you can easily put into words. There's a certain magic in the way he sings, a blend of technical mastery and emotional sincerity that's hard to find. It's the kind of voice that gets under your skin, that stays with you long after the song has ended. Cole had a gift for making every song feel like it was written just for you, and that's something I've always strived to do in my own performances.

Listening to Nat King Cole, I'm reminded of the power of subtlety. In a world that often values volume and spectacle, Cole's voice was a reminder that sometimes, less is more. Crooning is, at its heart, about restraint, about knowing when to hold back, when to let the music breathe, when to let a note linger just long enough to make its impact. Cole understood this better than almost anyone, and his music is a masterclass in the art of less is more.

Nat King Cole's influence on the world of crooning is immeasurable. He showed us all that crooning isn't just about technique or style, it's about heart. It's about creating a connection, about making the listener feel something real and true. And that's what Cole did, time and time again. His music continues to inspire new generations of singers, and his legacy as one of the greatest crooners of all time is secure.

For me, Nat King Cole will always be a touchstone, a reminder of what it means to truly connect with an audience. When I walk up to the microphone, I sometimes think about Cole's voice, about the way he could take a simple song and turn it into something magical. It's a gift, and one that I hope to carry with me in my own journey as a crooner.

CHAPTER 10: THE EVOLUTION OF CROONING IN MODERN MUSIC

As the decades rolled on, the world of music changed dramatically. New genres emerged, technology advanced, and the tastes of listeners evolved. Yet, even as rock and roll, disco, and electronic music took the spotlight, crooning never truly disappeared. Its intimate, emotionally rich style remained a touchstone for singers and listeners alike. Over time, the essence of crooning continued to evolve, finding its way into new genres and inspiring generations of artists who, while perhaps not always thought of as traditional crooners, embodied the spirit of the style.

The first modern artist who comes to mind whenever I think about crooning's evolution is Harry Connick Jr. In the late 1980s and early 1990s, Connick burst onto the scene with a sound that was equal parts jazz, swing, and pop, with a healthy dose of crooning at its core. His breakout work on the soundtrack for When Harry Met Sally... introduced a new generation of listeners to the sounds of classic standards like It Had to Be You and Let's

Call the Whole Thing Off. Connick had that natural crooner ability to make every song feel intimate, even when backed by a full orchestra. His phrasing, his relaxed delivery, and the way he could breathe new life into old standards, all of it harked back to the golden age of crooning, while still sounding fresh and modern.

What Connick did so brilliantly was blend the timeless qualities of crooning with a more contemporary sensibility. He wasn't just imitating Sinatra or Crosby, he was bringing something of himself to the music, honouring the tradition while pushing it forward. His voice, smooth and full of charm, had that effortless quality that all great crooners possess, but he also had a sense of fun, a playfulness in his performances that set him apart from the legends of the past. In a world where pop music was dominated by synths and heavy production, Connick's approach felt like a breath of fresh air. He wasn't afraid to be understated, to let the music do the talking. And audiences loved him for it.

Of course, no conversation about modern crooning would be complete without mentioning Michael Bublé. If there's any artist who has successfully carried the crooning torch into the 21st century, it's Bublé. From the moment he released his self-titled debut album in 2003, it was clear that Bublé wasn't just another pop singer, he was a crooner for the new millennium. His voice, rich and expressive, had that same effortless quality that defined the greats. Whether he was singing a classic like Come Fly With Me or a more contemporary tune like Home, Bublé had a way of making every song feel personal, as though he was singing just for you.

What's been particularly impressive about Bublé is his ability to straddle the line between tradition and modernity. He's never been afraid to embrace the old standards, but he's also carved out his own space in the music world with original songs that have that same crooning heart. Tracks like 'Haven't Met You Yet' and 'Everything' show that crooning doesn't have to be stuck in the past, it can evolve, it can grow, and it can still resonate with today's audiences. Bublé's success is a testament to the enduring appeal of crooning. Even in an age dominated by hip-hop and indie rock, there's still a place for the smooth, romantic sounds of a crooner.

Bublé's popularity has also highlighted something important about crooning, it's not just for the older generations. His music appeals to listeners of all ages, from those who grew up listening to Sinatra and Tony Bennett to younger audiences who might be discovering the style for the first time. That's the beauty of crooning, it's timeless. No matter what musical trends come and go, there will always be something special about a voice that can tell a story, that can make you feel like you're the only one in the room.

Beyond Connick and Bublé, there are plenty of other artists who've taken the crooning tradition and made it their own. Artists like John Mayer, with his laid-back vocal style, often tap into the intimate, conversational qualities that define crooning. His hit Gravity, for instance, has that same emotional weight and subtlety that you'd find in a classic crooner ballad. Mayer doesn't necessarily fit into the traditional mold of a crooner, but the influence is there in the way he approaches his vocals, in the way he uses his voice to tell a story.

Even in the world of rock and indie music, you can hear echoes of crooning. Artists like Alex Turner of Arctic Monkeys have occasionally leaned into the style, particularly on albums like Tranquility Base Hotel & Casino, where Turner's voice takes on a smooth, almost lounge-singer quality. It's a reminder that crooning isn't confined to one genre, it's a way of using the voice that can fit into any musical context. The same can be said for Lana Del Rey, whose dreamy, nostalgic sound often calls to mind the lush, cinematic feel of classic crooning.

As music continues to evolve, crooning has found a place in the digital age as well. Artists like Sam Smith and Adele, while not traditional crooners in the strictest sense, often incorporate the emotional sincerity and vocal control that are hallmarks of the style. Adele, in particular, has a voice that's capable of conveying deep emotion with a kind of restraint that feels very much in line with the crooning tradition. Her ballads, like Someone Like You and When We Were Young, have that same heart-wrenching quality that you'd expect from a classic crooner tune. It's not about vocal fireworks, it's about delivering the song with honesty and vulnerability.

In some ways, the digital age has been a blessing for crooners. With platforms like YouTube and streaming services, artists don't need to rely on traditional radio or record labels to find an audience. A new generation of crooners, inspired by the likes of Sinatra, Bennett, and Cole, are emerging online, using social media and digital platforms to share their music with the world. It's proof that the art of crooning is still very much alive, even in a world where the music industry looks completely different than it did 50 or 60 years ago.

One of the things I've found most inspiring about modern crooning is the way it continues to adapt while staying true to its core. At its heart, crooning is about the voice. It's about using the voice to connect with the listener, to make them feel something real and true. And that's something that will never go out of style. Whether it's a traditional jazz standard or a contemporary pop ballad, the principles of crooning, sincerity, restraint, emotional depth, remain as relevant as ever.

For me, as a crooner, it's exciting to see how this style continues to evolve. I've always believed that crooning isn't about trying to sound like the past, it's about taking the lessons of the greats and applying them to the music of today. When I perform, I'm not just thinking about Sinatra or Bennett, I'm thinking about how I can use my voice to create a connection, to tell a story, to make the audience feel something. That's what crooning has always been about, and that's why it continues to endure.

As I look to the future, I'm confident that crooning will continue to find its place in modern music. The landscape may change, and the trends may shift, but there will always be a place for a voice that can move people, that can speak to the heart. And as long as there are singers who understand the power of that connection, crooning will never truly fade away.

CHAPTER 11: MEETING TONY BENNETT IN MANCHESTER

There are certain moments in life that stay with you forever, moments where the stars align and you find yourself face-to-face with someone who has shaped your life in ways you never imagined. For me, one of those moments came when I had the incredible opportunity to meet Tony Bennett at the Bridgewater Hall in Manchester. It wasn't just a fleeting encounter with a famous singer, it was the culmination of years of admiration, of studying his music, of being inspired by his voice, his artistry, and the way he lived his life as a musician.

Tony Bennett had always been a towering figure in my life as a crooner. From the moment I first heard his voice, with its effortless grace and emotional depth, I was hooked. There was something about Tony's approach to music that resonated deeply with me. He wasn't just singing songs, he was telling stories, painting pictures with his voice, and making you feel like you were a part of something intimate and personal. His influence on my own singing can't be overstated. I studied his phrasing, his timing, the way he could hold back just enough to make you hang on every word, and then, when the moment was right, let the full weight of the emotion come through.

So, when my wife, Val told me that Tony Bennett would be performing at the Bridgewater Hall in Manchester, she knew I wouldn't want to miss the chance to see him live and had bought us tickets as a suprise. The prospect of watching him perform in person, in my homecity no less, felt almost surreal. I had followed his career for so long, listened to his records, watched his performances, and now, here he was, right on my doorstep.

The Bridgewater Hall is a stunning venue, renowned for its acoustics and its ability to create an intimate atmosphere despite its size. Walking through its doors that evening, there was a palpable sense of excitement in the air. The audience, a mix of fans who had been following Tony's career for decades and younger listeners who had discovered him more recently, buzzed with anticipation. For many of us, this was a once-in-a-lifetime opportunity to witness a legend at work, to hear that unmistakable voice fill the hall with the songs we had come to love.

As I sat in the audience waiting for the show to begin, I felt a mixture of emotions, excitement, certainly, but also a kind of nervousness, as though I was about to meet an old friend for the first time in ages. I had spent so much time with Tony's voice over the years that it felt like I already knew him, like he had been a part of my life for as long as I could remember. And yet, here he was, in the flesh, ready to step out onto the stage and bring those songs to life right in front of me.

When Tony Bennett finally appeared on stage, the audience erupted in applause, a wave of love and admiration that washed over him as he smiled graciously and took his place at the microphone. And then, with that first note, the room seemed to stop. There's something about hearing a voice like Tony Bennett's live that you can't quite capture in a recording. It's not just the sound, it's the presence, the way he commands the room without ever raising his voice, the way he makes every person in the audience feel like he's singing just for them.

For the next hour or so, I was completely transfixed. Tony's set was a mix of classics and personal favourites, each one delivered with that signature warmth and sincerity that had made him a legend. Whether he was singing The Way You Look Tonight or Fly Me to the Moon, there was an effortlessness to his performance, a sense that he was as comfortable on that stage as he would have been in his own living room. And yet, there was also a deep respect for the music, for the audience, for the moment. Tony never took it for granted, every note, every phrase was crafted with care, with love, with a sense of responsibility to the song and to the people who had come to hear him.

But what struck me most that night wasn't just Tony's voice or his performance, it was his humility. Here was a man who had spent decades at the top of his game, who had sung with everyone from Frank Sinatra to Lady Gaga, who had won countless awards and accolades, and yet he carried himself with such grace, such humility. There was no ego, no pretense, just a deep love for the music and for the people who had come to share in it with him.

After the show, I had the unbelievable privilege of meeting Tony in person. I wasn't aware but Val had arranged it beforehand with his management for me to meet him. It was one of those moments where you find yourself wondering if it's really happening, if you're really standing face-to-face with someone who has been such a huge influence in your life. I was nervous, of course, what do you say to a man like Tony Bennett? How do you put into words the impact he's had on your own journey as a singer, as a crooner?

But Tony, being the gracious man that he is, immediately put me at ease. He greeted me with a smile, and for a moment, I felt like I was in the presence of an old friend rather than a world-famous singer. We spoke briefly, and I told him how much his music had meant to me, how his voice had been a guiding light for me as I developed my own career as a crooner. I'll never forget the kindness in his eyes, the way he listened intently, as though my words truly mattered to him.

In that brief conversation, Tony shared a few words of encouragement that have stayed with me ever since. He spoke about the importance of staying true to the music, of letting the songs speak for themselves, and of always performing with sincerity. It wasn't about fame or fortune, he said, it was about connecting with people, about using your voice to bring something real and meaningful into the world. That's what crooning had always been for Tony, and it's what it has become for me as well.

Meeting Tony Bennett that night was more than just a thrill, it was a confirmation that I was on the right path, that the journey I had embarked on as a crooner was one worth pursuing. Tony had always been an example to me of what it meant to be a true artist, someone who never lost sight of the music, who never compromised his integrity, and who always put the audience first. And in that moment, standing there with him, I felt a renewed sense of purpose, a reminder of why I do what I do.

The memory of that night at the Bridgewater Hall will always be a special one for me. It was a chance to not only see one of my heroes in action, but to connect with him on a personal level, to share a moment of mutual respect and understanding. Tony Bennett has given so much to the world through his music, and I'm grateful to have had the opportunity to express to him, even if only for a brief moment, what his voice has meant to me.

Every time I step onto the stage now, I carry that moment with me. It's a reminder of the power of music, of the importance of staying true to the craft, and of the gift that is being able to share a song with an audience. Tony Bennett taught me that crooning isn't just about singing, it's about creating a connection, about using your voice to bring something beautiful into the world. And for that, I will always be grateful.

CHAPTER 12: THE ALZHEIMER'S FUNDRAISER: SINGING FOR 24 HOURS

When Tony Bennett announced that he was living with Alzheimer's disease, it struck me on a profoundly personal level. Here was a man who had given so much to the world, through his music, his voice, his spirit, now facing one of the cruellest diseases. It felt as though the world was losing a piece of its soul, the smooth elegance of his voice being slowly dimmed by something beyond anyone's control. I knew then that I wanted to do something, something meaningful, to honour Tony, to give back to him in a small way for all the years of inspiration he'd given me.

That's how the idea for the 24-hour non-stop singing marathon was born. It was one of those moments where inspiration hits you like a bolt of lightning. I knew I wanted to raise funds for the Alzheimer's Society, to help support those living with the disease and their families, and I wanted to do it in Tony's honour. But more than that, I wanted the act of fundraising itself to reflect what Tony had meant to me as a crooner, as someone who had dedicated his life to music. It had to be something challenging, something that pushed me beyond my limits, just as Tony had always pushed himself to reach new heights in his career. Tony's wife Susan, said in an interview that Alzheimer's is a 24 hour a day condition but music really helps Tony. That's when I decided to combine the music with 24 hours. I would sing non-stop for 24 hours in Tony's honour.

It was an ambitious plan, no doubt about it. Singing for 24 hours straight isn't just a physical challenge, it's a mental and emotional one as well. But that's exactly why it felt like the right thing to do. Tony had given his heart and soul to his music for over 70 years, and this was my way of giving something back, of showing my appreciation and support for him in the best way I knew how, through song.

As the day of the marathon approached, I began to prepare myself both mentally and physically. I trained my voice, building up stamina, ensuring that I could go the distance without losing my tone or strength. I practised hour after hour, learning to pace myself, to manage my energy so that I could sustain my performance over the full 24 hours. But no matter how much I prepared, I knew that once I was in the thick of it, it would come down to sheer willpower and determination.

On the day of the marathon, I arrived at the venue, Mulino Restaurant in Urmston, Manchester, it was shut due to the Covid-19 lockdown, so I had the place to myself. I had a sliding window where people could come to donate. I was feeling a mixture of excitement and nerves. I had done everything I could to prepare, but there's only so much you can do to brace yourself for something like this. The room was set up with microphones, bottles of water, and a rotating group of supporters who would cheer me on and keep the energy going throughout the day and night. In many ways, this wasn't just about me, it was a communal effort, with people from all walks of life coming together to support a cause that was close to all our hearts.

The press got wind of what I was up to. BBC North West Tonight came along and interviewed me before I started. Irish TV also filmed me preparing to start the marathon. The Irish Post Newspaper along with The Messenger Newspaper and the Manchester Evening News all ran features on what I was doing. It brought attention to my cause, to salute Tony and to raise funds for the Alzheimer's Society.

The first few hours flew by, as I sang through classic standards, ballads, and upbeat numbers, each one dedicated to Tony and the millions of others affected by Alzheimer's. It felt almost surreal, knowing that I was doing this for a man who had inspired me for so long, a man who, at that very moment, was facing the harsh realities of this devastating disease. But there was also a sense of peace in the music, a sense that, for these 24 hours, I was helping to keep Tony's legacy alive, not just in my own heart, but in the hearts of everyone who was supporting the fundraiser.

As the hours wore on, the challenge began to set in. Physically, my voice began to tire, and I could feel the strain of non-stop singing in my throat, my chest, and even in my body. My feet ached from standing for so long, and the hours seemed to stretch out ahead of me like a never-ending road. But I kept going, driven by the thought of Tony and the incredible work of the Alzheimer's Society, whose mission I so strongly believed in. Every song I sang felt like a small tribute to those affected by the disease, a reminder that even in the face of something as difficult as Alzheimer's, there was still beauty to be found in the music.

By the time I reached the halfway point, 12 hours in, I was exhausted, but I had hit my stride. There's something about pushing through that wall of fatigue that changes the way you experience time. The hours began to blur together, and I found myself entering a kind of rhythm, my voice carrying me from song to song, from standard to standard. At some point, the physical discomfort faded into the background, and it became less about my own endurance and more about the music, about the cause, about honouring Tony and raising awareness for Alzheimer's.

One of the most powerful moments of the marathon came when I received a message that Tony Bennett himself had shared my fundraising effort on his social media channels. To know that Tony was aware of what I was doing, to know that he had taken the time to highlight my efforts to his millions of followers, meant the world to me. It was as if everything I had worked for, the years of singing, of studying his music, of being inspired by his voice, had come full circle. Tony, the man who had given so much to me and to countless others through his music, was now recognising my small act of tribute to him. It was a moment I will never forget.

As the marathon entered its final stretch, I could feel the fatigue creeping back in. My voice was raw, my body aching, but I knew I couldn't stop now. I had come this far, and there was no turning back. I was surrounded by friends, family, and supporters, and as always my wife, Val, always at my side, all of whom had been there with me through the long hours, cheering me on and reminding me why I was doing this. Their energy kept me going, even when I thought I had nothing left to give.

Finally, after what felt like an eternity, the 24th hour arrived. As I sang my final song, My Way, a fitting tribute to Tony Bennett, the weight of the moment hit me. I had done it. I had sung non-stop for 24 hours, raised funds for the Alzheimer's Society, and, in my own small way, honoured Tony Bennett and his incredible legacy. There was a sense of deep satisfaction, not just in having completed the marathon, but in knowing that I had used my voice, the very thing Tony had inspired me to develop, to make a difference.

But the most emotional moment of all came after the marathon was over, when I received a personal letter from Tony Bennett himself. In it, he thanked me for my efforts, for the fundraising, for honouring him in such a meaningful way. He didn't have to write that letter, he didn't have to acknowledge my marathon at all, but that's the kind of man Tony was. Gracious, kind, humble, always thinking of others. That letter is something I will treasure for the rest of my life, a reminder of the incredible connection music can create between people, even across generations and across oceans.

And then, as if the experience couldn't get any more surreal, I received a phone call from Tony Bennett. Hearing his voice on the other end of the line, thanking me personally for what I had done, was a moment of pure emotion. Here was the man who had inspired my entire career as a crooner, calling me to express his gratitude for something I had done in his honour. I was overwhelmed, humbled, and deeply moved. It felt like the culmination of everything I had worked for as a singer, as a performer, and as someone who had spent years studying the art of crooning.

The 24-hour singing marathon was one of the hardest things I've ever done, both physically and emotionally. But it was also one of the most rewarding. It was a chance to give back to someone who had given me so much, and to raise awareness for a cause that affects so many lives. Every time I think back on that experience, I'm reminded of the power of music to heal, to connect, and to make a difference in the world.

And every time I step up to the microphone now, I carry that memory with me. It's a reminder of why I sing, of why I do what I do, not for fame or recognition, but for the love of the music, for the connection it creates, and for the way it can touch people's lives, just as Tony Bennett has touched mine.

Tony Bennett ✓
3 m · 🌐

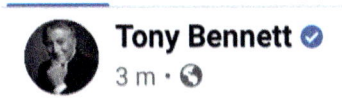

Thanks again to Wayne Devlin & congratulations on 612 songs, 24 hours of singing, and £8k raised for Alzheimer's Society.

"I don't try to impersonate Tony when I sing, no one could do it how he does, but I sing his songs in my own voice to salute him out of respect and admiration."

Tony Bennett ✓
26 Feb · 🌐

Absolutely inspiring to see fans making a change in the world. Keep it up, Wayne Devlin.
Learn about his 24-hour Swing-A-Thon in support of Alzheimer's Society, and find out how to donate here: www.justgiving.com/fundraising/Wayne-Devlin

Wayne Devlin's

24 HOUR SWING-A-THON
in aid of Alzheimer's Society
www.justgiving.com/fundraising/Wayne-Devlin

"

After learning that music really helps Tony and that living with Alzheimers is a 24 hour a day thing, I decided I wanted to do something to raise awareness here in the UK and also to salute my hero Tony Bennett and **let him know how much we care about him** and how much we love him for being the soundtrack to our lives.

"

www.justgiving.com/fundraising/Wayne-Devlin

WAYNEDEVLINBCAA

10 DOWNING STREET
LONDON SW1A 2AA

THE PRIME MINISTER

17 March 2021

Dear Wayne,

Thank you for your recent 24 hour 'Swing-a-thon' in honour of the great Tony Bennett. Music is incredibly therapeutic for dementia sufferers and your soothing crooning will have brought joy and calm to many living with the disease.

The funds you have raised will also help to further pioneering research into dementia. This, in addition to the £500,000 you have raised over the last decade, will have a huge impact on people's lives.

On behalf of all those you have helped, thank you, and congratulations on becoming the UK's 1624th Point of Light.

Wayne Devlin

CHAPTER 13: TONY BENNETT'S RESPONSE: A PERSONAL THANK YOU

There are moments in life that shift your perspective, moments that remind you why you do what you do and why you've chosen to walk the path you're on. One of those moments for me came after I completed my 24-hour non-stop singing marathon to raise funds for the Alzheimer's Society in honour of Tony Bennett. I had undertaken the challenge with the hope of contributing something meaningful, something that could make a difference in the lives of those affected by Alzheimer's. I had pushed myself to the limit, driven by my admiration for Tony Bennett and my desire to show my support for him during his battle with the disease. But nothing could have prepared me for what came next.

I had known that Tony Bennett's team was aware of my fundraiser. When they highlighted my efforts on his social media channels, it was already more than I could have ever expected.

The thought of Tony himself knowing about what I was doing, of him taking a moment to share my story with his followers, filled me with a sense of pride and gratitude that was hard to put into words. It felt like everything had come full circle, like I was somehow giving back to a man who had given so much to me over the years through his music and his artistry.

But then came the letter. I'll never forget the day it arrived, a handwritten note from Tony Bennett himself, thanking me for what I had done. I was speechless. Here was a man who had performed for royalty, for presidents, for millions of fans all over the world, taking the time to sit down and write to me, thanking me for a fundraiser I had organised in his honour. It was one of the most humbling moments of my life.

The letter was simple, but its impact was profound. Tony thanked me for singing for 24 hours to raise awareness and funds for the Alzheimer's Society. He expressed his appreciation for the effort and the dedication it took to complete such a gruelling challenge. But more than that, he spoke about the importance of community, of how music can bring people together, even in the face of something as difficult as Alzheimer's. He thanked me for using my voice to make a difference, for showing solidarity with those who are battling the disease, and for honouring him in such a meaningful way.

As I read those words, I felt an overwhelming sense of connection, not just to Tony, but to the larger community of musicians, supporters, and caregivers who had come together to support the cause. It was a reminder that music has the power to heal, to inspire, and to bring hope, even in the darkest of times. Tony's letter wasn't just a thank-you note; it was a testament to the impact that music can have on people's lives. It reminded me that, as a singer, I had the ability to touch people's hearts, to make a difference in ways that went far beyond the stage.

But the story didn't end with the letter. Not long after, I received a phone call, one that I will never forget for as long as I live. On the other end of the line was Tony Bennett himself. I could hardly believe it. Tony Bennett, one of the greatest voices of all time, the man who had inspired my entire career, was calling me to thank me personally. It was a surreal moment, one that I had never imagined could happen, and yet, here it was, unfolding in real time.

Hearing Tony's voice on the phone was an emotional experience. There was something about the way he spoke, the kindness and sincerity in his words, that brought everything full circle for me. He didn't just thank me for the fundraiser, he took the time to ask how I was, to talk about the importance of raising awareness for Alzheimer's, and to share a few words of encouragement. It was as though he understood the emotional weight of the challenge I had undertaken, and he wanted me to know just how much it meant to him.

I could feel the connection between us, even across the distance. Tony's words were gracious, heartfelt, and deeply personal. He spoke about the power of music to bring people together, about the importance of using one's voice for good, and about the strength of the community that had supported him throughout his battle with Alzheimer's. I was struck by his humility, by the way he spoke with such gratitude and grace, even as he faced one of the most difficult challenges of his life.

In that conversation, I realised that this wasn't just about music or fundraising, it was about humanity. It was about the connections we make with one another, the ways in which we support each other through difficult times, and the role that music can play in bringing us closer together. Tony Bennett had always been a beacon of light in the world of music, but in that moment, he became something even more for me, a symbol of resilience, of kindness, and of the enduring power of the human spirit.

That phone call was more than just a conversation, it was

a moment of deep emotional connection, one that reaffirmed everything I believed about the power of music and the importance of community. Tony's words stayed with me long after I hung up the phone, and they continue to inspire me every time I step onto the stage. Knowing that he took the time to reach out to me, to express his gratitude, was a reminder of the profound impact that one person's voice can have on the world.

But it wasn't just Tony's personal acknowledgment that left a lasting impression on me, it was the knowledge that my small act of tribute had resonated with him in such a meaningful way. To have the opportunity to give something back to the man who had shaped my career, who had been a source of inspiration for me from the very beginning, was an honour I will carry with me for the rest of my life. It reminded me that, as artists, we are part of something bigger than ourselves. We are part of a tradition, a community of voices that spans generations, and every time we perform, we are contributing to that legacy.

Tony's response to my fundraiser wasn't just a personal victory, it was a reminder of why I do what I do. It reinforced the idea that music has the power to change lives, to bring people together, and to create moments of connection that transcend the boundaries of time and space. Whether I'm singing in a small club or on a larger stage, I carry that knowledge with me, and it pushes me to give my all, every time.

For me, that phone call from Tony Bennett was the culmination of years of admiration, of study, of love for the art of crooning. It was a moment that tied together my own journey as a crooner with the legacy that Tony has built over decades of performing. It was a reminder that, at the heart of it all, music is about connection, it's about reaching out to others and creating something that speaks to the soul.

Tony's words of encouragement have stayed with me, a constant reminder that the path I'm on is the right one. Every time I perform, I think back to that letter, to that phone call, to the kindness and grace that Tony showed me, and it fuels me to keep going, to keep singing, to keep using my voice to bring people together. That's what Tony had done throughout his entire career, and it's what I hope to continue doing in my own.

The experience of raising funds in Tony's honour, of receiving his personal acknowledgment, has become one of the defining moments of my career. It has given me a renewed sense of purpose, a reminder of why I fell in love with crooning in the first place, and a deep appreciation for the power of music to heal, to inspire, and to bring joy to others. And for that, I will always be grateful to Tony Bennett, not just for his music, but for the way he has touched my life and the lives of so many others.

CHAPTER 14: THE WOMEN OF CROONING

When people talk about crooning, the first names that often come to mind are the big male stars, Sinatra, Crosby, Bennett. And while these men undoubtedly helped define the genre, it's important to remember that the art of crooning wouldn't be what it is today without the remarkable contributions of female crooners. The women of crooning brought something unique to the style, something that expanded the emotional range and depth of the music. They infused the genre with elegance, grace, and often a vulnerability that spoke to listeners on a different level.

One of the most iconic female crooners, and a true pioneer of the style, was Billie Holiday. Though often associated with jazz, Billie's soft, intimate vocal delivery had all the hallmarks of classic crooning. There was something haunting in the way she sang, as though every note carried the weight of her experiences, her pain, and her resilience. Songs like God Bless the Child and Strange Fruit were more than just performances, they were deeply personal expressions of her life, her struggles, and her observations of the world around her.

Billie's voice wasn't technically perfect in the traditional sense, it wasn't the kind of polished, showy vocal you might hear from some of her contemporaries. But that's exactly what made her so special. There was a rawness to her singing, a sense that she was speaking directly from her soul. And like the best crooners, she knew how to take a song and make it her own, bringing a level of emotion and intimacy that drew listeners in. Even when singing upbeat numbers, there was always an undercurrent of melancholy in Billie's voice, a reminder that the stories she was telling were rooted in real-life experiences. In many ways, Billie Holiday embodied the very essence of crooning, the ability to convey deep emotion with subtlety, to create a connection that went beyond mere entertainment.

Another towering figure in the world of female crooners was Peggy Lee. Unlike Billie Holiday, Peggy had a voice that was pure silk, smooth, controlled, and endlessly versatile. Her style was sophisticated, almost understated, but with a powerful emotional core that resonated in every song she sang. Peggy's crooning was the kind that could make you feel warm and comforted, yet also make you ache with longing. Songs like Fever and Is That All There Is? showed her incredible ability to control the atmosphere of a song, to shift from playful to serious in the blink of an eye.

One of the things that always struck me about Peggy Lee was her mastery of restraint. She understood the power of what wasn't said, of the spaces between the notes, of letting the listener fill in the emotional gaps. She didn't need to belt out a tune to make her point, her quiet, sultry delivery was enough to make you hang on every word. That's a hallmark of great crooning, the ability to create tension and anticipation through subtlety. Peggy was a master of that art, and her influence on modern female vocalists can still be heard today.

Moving beyond Peggy Lee, it's impossible to talk about female crooners without mentioning the incomparable Ella Fitzgerald.

Known as the "First Lady of Song," Ella's voice was something truly special, crystal clear, pitch-perfect, and capable of handling anything from delicate ballads to swinging jazz numbers. But what made Ella such an extraordinary crooner was her ability to blend technical perfection with emotional depth. Every note she sang was flawless, but it was never just about the notes. Ella had a way of making every song feel fresh, like you were hearing it for the first time, even if it was a classic you'd listened to a thousand times before.

Ella's crooning was elegant, graceful, and full of life. She could take a simple love song and turn it into a masterpiece of emotion, using her voice to convey the joy, the excitement, and the heartbreak of falling in and out of love. Songs like Misty and Someone to Watch Over Me are perfect examples of how she could transform a melody, infusing it with warmth, sincerity, and a sense of wonder. When Ella crooned, she didn't just sing to you, she invited you into her world, letting you feel the emotions she was feeling, even if only for the duration of the song.

While Billie, Peggy, and Ella were giants in the world of crooning, there were countless other women who contributed to the style, each bringing their own unique voice to the tradition. Sarah Vaughan, for instance, had a voice that was rich and full-bodied, with a deep warmth that made every song feel like a personal confession. Her control over her instrument was astonishing, she could glide effortlessly between registers, shifting from a velvety low note to a soaring high note with ease. Sarah's crooning had a kind of drama to it, a sense that every song was a story being told not just with words, but with every inflection, every breath.

Then there was Dinah Washington, whose voice was like no other, brassy, bold, but still capable of moments of tenderness and vulnerability. Dinah's style was a bit more forceful than some of her contemporaries, but that didn't mean she lacked the ability to croon. In fact, her renditions of songs like What a Difference a Day Made and This Bitter Earth showcased her ability to draw out the emotional core of a song, to make the listener feel every ounce of heartache or joy she was expressing. Dinah's voice had a way of cutting through everything else, reaching straight into your heart and leaving a lasting impression.

What all of these women had in common, despite their different styles and approaches, was their ability to make you feel something real. That's what crooning is all about, and it's why the contributions of female crooners are just as important as those of their male counterparts. They brought their own unique perspectives to the music, often infusing it with a depth of emotion that added new layers to the songs they sang.

Even today, the influence of these female crooners can be heard in the voices of modern artists. Singers like Norah Jones, Diana Krall, and even Adele carry on the tradition of crooning, using their voices to create moments of intimacy and connection with their listeners. Norah Jones, with her soft, breathy vocals and understated delivery, often feels like a modern-day Peggy Lee, while Diana Krall's jazz-inflected style has echoes of Ella Fitzgerald's precision and grace. Adele, though more known for her powerhouse ballads, still taps into the emotional vulnerability that defined singers like Billie Holiday, using her voice to tell stories of love, loss, and longing.

As a crooner myself, I've often found inspiration in the work of these incredible women. Their ability to bring nuance and depth to every performance, to make each song feel like a personal conversation with the listener, is something I strive to emulate in my own singing. They showed me that crooning isn't just about vocal technique, it's about heart, about soul, about using your voice to connect with people in a way that transcends time and place.

The women of crooning have left an indelible mark on the music world, and their contributions continue to inspire new generations of singers. They remind us that crooning isn't confined to any one gender or style, it's about creating an emotional connection, about telling a story with your voice, and about bringing something of yourself to every song you sing. Whether it's Billie's raw vulnerability, Peggy's elegant restraint, or Ella's joyful exuberance, these women have shown us all what it means to truly croon.

CHAPTER 15: THE DECLINE OF CROONING IN THE 1970S AND 1980S

By the time the 1970s rolled around, the world of music was changing at a rapid pace. The smooth, intimate sounds of crooning that had once dominated the airwaves began to fade as new genres like rock, disco, and eventually electronic music took centre stage. It was an era defined by experimentation, rebellion, and a desire to push boundaries, and crooning, rooted in emotional nuance and subtlety, found itself somewhat out of step with the times.

The 1960s had already seen a significant shift in popular music with the rise of rock and roll. Artists like The Beatles, The Rolling Stones, and Bob Dylan had changed the landscape entirely, bringing a raw energy and youthful rebellion that appealed to a new generation of listeners. This trend continued into the 1970s, as rock music became more experimental and ambitious, with the emergence of subgenres like progressive rock, glam rock, and eventually, punk rock. The music of this era was louder, more confrontational, and, in many ways, more reflective of the social and political turmoil of the time.

Crooning, with its emphasis on romance, tenderness, and emotional vulnerability, didn't quite fit into the new musical narrative. The big band arrangements and jazz-influenced melodies that had defined the genre felt almost nostalgic in an era when electric guitars and synthesizers were the instruments of choice. The contrast between the rebellious spirit of rock and roll and the sentimental elegance of crooning couldn't have been more stark.

As a result, many of the great crooners of the previous decades found themselves somewhat sidelined. Frank Sinatra, for instance, had been a dominant figure in popular music throughout the 1940s and 1950s, but by the 1970s, even he was facing challenges in maintaining his relevance. His 1970 album Watertown, an ambitious concept album, was a commercial failure, and although he continued to perform and record throughout the decade, his style of music was no longer at the forefront of the popular imagination.

Tony Bennett, too, faced a difficult period during the 1970s. The public's taste had shifted, and the kind of music that Bennett excelled at, standards, jazz ballads, and classic pop songs, was no longer in demand. By the mid-1970s, Bennett had parted ways with his record label and was struggling to find his footing in a music industry that seemed to have left crooning behind. In fact, it wasn't until much later in his career that Bennett would experience a resurgence, thanks to his commitment to staying true to his roots and the rediscovery of his music by younger generations, thanks to the fantastic and somewhat genius management guidance of his career by his son Danny.

For many other crooners, the 1970s and 1980s marked the twilight of their careers. The cultural shift toward louder, more aggressive forms of music, whether it was the raw energy of punk or the flashy spectacle of disco, left little room for the kind of quiet, introspective singing that crooning represented. The disco craze of the late 1970s, in particular, was emblematic of a music scene that valued rhythm, energy, and danceability over emotional storytelling and subtle vocal performances. Artists like Donna Summer and The Bee Gees dominated the charts with their upbeat, high-energy hits, while crooning seemed increasingly out of place in the musical landscape.

Even in the world of jazz, where crooning had its roots, changes were afoot. Fusion jazz, blending elements of jazz with rock, funk, and electronic music, became popular in the 1970s, as artists like Miles Davis and Herbie Hancock began to experiment with new sounds and technologies. This was a far cry from the big band jazz and swing that had once provided the perfect backdrop for crooners like Sinatra and Bennett. The traditional crooning style, with its lush orchestral arrangements and romantic melodies, seemed to belong to another era.

Of course, this doesn't mean that crooning disappeared entirely during the 1970s and 1980s. Many crooners continued to perform live, maintaining devoted fan bases that spanned generations. Sinatra, for instance, remained a beloved live performer throughout the 1970s and into the 1980s, his concerts still drawing huge crowds of adoring fans. The same was true for other crooners like Tony Bennett and Perry Como, whose live performances provided a welcome respite from the frenetic energy of rock and disco. There was always an audience for crooning, even if it wasn't the audience that dominated the charts.

But it's also worth noting that, while crooning may have been on the decline in terms of commercial success, its influence could still be felt in the music of the time. Many of the best songwriters of the 1970s and 1980s, people like Elton John, Billy Joel, and even Paul McCartney, were clearly influenced by the melodic structures and emotional depth of classic crooning. Songs like Elton John's Your Song or Billy Joel's Just the Way You Are may not be crooning in the traditional sense, but they carry the same emotional weight and sincerity that defined the genre.

In fact, it could be argued that crooning never really left, it simply evolved. The essence of crooning, that intimate connection between singer and listener, that emotional vulnerability, was still very much alive in the ballads and love songs of the 1970s and 1980s. Artists like Barbra Streisand and Barry Manilow, for example, carried the torch for romantic balladry during this period, bringing a modern sensibility to the kind of heartfelt performances that crooners had perfected in the decades before.

And then, of course, there were the late-career resurgences of some of the great crooners. Frank Sinatra, after a brief period of semi-retirement in the early 1970s, came back in a big way with his 1980 album Trilogy: Past Present Future. The album featured Theme from New York, New York, a song that would go on to become one of his signature hits and an anthem for the city. It was a reminder that, while crooning may not have been at the centre of the musical zeitgeist, it still had the power to captivate audiences.

For Tony Bennett, the 1980s marked a turning point in his career as well. After struggling through much of the 1970s, Bennett made a conscious decision to return to the Great American Songbook and to focus on what he did best: singing standards with heart, soul, and authenticity. His efforts paid off, and by the end of the 1980s, he was experiencing a renaissance that would carry him through the 1990s and into the 21st century.

As a crooner myself, looking back at this period of musical history is a reminder that every genre goes through cycles. There are times when a particular style is at the forefront of popular culture, and there are times when it recedes into the background, making way for new trends and innovations. But even during those quieter moments, the essence of crooning never truly disappears. It remains in the DNA of so much of the music we love, whether we recognise it or not.

The 1970s and 1980s may have been a difficult time for crooners in terms of commercial success, but the music itself, those timeless songs of love, loss, and longing, endured. And, as we would see in the decades to come, crooning wasn't gone forever. It was simply waiting for the right moment to return to the spotlight.

CHAPTER 16: THE REVIVAL OF CROONING: FROM HARRY CONNICK JR. TO MICHAEL BUBLÉ

By the time the 1990s rolled around, crooning, which had taken a backseat to other genres throughout much of the 1970s and 1980s, was ready for a comeback. It's often said that everything old becomes new again, and crooning was no exception. The music industry and audiences alike began to crave something different, something that could balance the fast-paced, highly produced sounds of contemporary pop music. And so, crooning, rooted in simplicity, intimacy, and timeless melodies, returned to the mainstream, bringing with it a sense of nostalgia and class that felt refreshingly new in the midst of modern musical trends.

One of the key figures responsible for this revival was Harry Connick Jr. Bursting onto the scene in the late 1980s and early 1990s, Connick quickly became the torchbearer for a new generation of crooners. His soundtrack for the 1989 film When

Harry Met Sally... catapulted him to fame, with songs like It Had to Be You introducing a whole new audience to the sounds of classic standards. Connick's smooth vocals, combined with his jazz-inflected piano playing, brought the golden era of crooning back into the public consciousness, but with a fresh twist that felt contemporary.

What Connick did so well was blend the old with the new. He wasn't trying to imitate Sinatra or Crosby, though their influence on his music was undeniable, but rather he brought his own personality and charm to the music. Connick's voice had that effortless quality that defines all great crooners, but he infused his performances with a sense of fun, a playfulness that made the music feel alive and relevant to the times. His charisma, both on stage and on screen, helped him connect with younger audiences who may not have been familiar with the original crooners, but who found themselves drawn to the timeless appeal of the style.

Through the 1990s, Connick's success continued to grow, as he released a string of albums that showcased his versatility as both a singer and a musician. Albums like We Are in Love and Blue Light, Red Light cemented his reputation as a modern-day crooner, while his live performances, full of energy, humour, and heart, helped to keep the spirit of crooning alive. Connick's ability to bridge the gap between jazz and pop, between old-school standards and modern sensibilities, made him one of the key figures in the crooning revival of the 1990s.

But it wasn't just Connick who was breathing new life into the crooning tradition during this period. In the early 2000s, another young singer came onto the scene, and it wasn't long before he was being hailed as the next great crooner. That singer, of course, was Michael Bublé.

From the moment Bublé released his self-titled debut album in 2003, it was clear that he was a natural crooner. His voice, warm and rich with emotion, had that classic quality that could easily transport you back to the days of Sinatra and Bennett, but it also had a freshness to it, something that made it feel modern and accessible to new audiences. Bublé's ability to take classic songs like Come Fly with Me and Fever and make them feel fresh again was nothing short of remarkable. He brought a youthful energy to the music, one that allowed younger generations to appreciate the timelessness of crooning while also making it feel relevant in the context of contemporary pop music.

What set Bublé apart, much like Connick before him, was his ability to straddle the line between tradition and modernity. He wasn't just a throwback to the old days of crooning—he was something new, someone who could respect the past while still looking forward. His original songs, like Haven't Met You Yet and Everything, had all the emotional depth and sincerity of a classic crooner ballad, but they were also catchy, upbeat, and designed for the modern pop charts.

Bublé's live performances were another key to his success. Like Sinatra, he had a way of commanding the stage with a combination of smooth vocals, wit, and charm. He understood that crooning wasn't just about singing, it was about creating a connection with the audience, about making every person in the room feel like they were being sung to directly. This was the essence of crooning, and Bublé had mastered it.

Through the 2000s and 2010s, Bublé continued to build on his success, becoming one of the most recognisable crooners of the modern era. His Christmas albums, in particular, became cultural touchstones, cementing his place as a modern-day successor to the great crooners of the past. But what's truly impressive about Bublé's career is how he has managed to keep crooning alive in a music industry that is constantly changing. Even as pop music continues to evolve, with new genres and trends emerging seemingly every day, Bublé has remained true to the core principles of crooning, emotion, connection, and sincerity.

Beyond Connick and Bublé, other artists have also contributed to the crooning revival in their own ways. Rod Stewart, for instance, who was best known for his rock and pop hits in the 1970s and 1980s, reinvented himself in the 2000s with his Great American Songbook series. These albums, which featured Stewart's interpretations of classic standards like The Way You Look Tonight and As Time Goes By, introduced a whole new audience to the music of the Great American Songbook. Stewart's raspy, distinctive voice may not have been traditionally associated with crooning, but his heartfelt delivery and respect for the material made these albums a success, showing once again that the appeal of crooning was universal.

And then there's Diana Krall, whose jazz-inflected vocal style has often drawn comparisons to the great female crooners of the past. Krall's albums, such as The Look of Love and Quiet Nights, are full of the kind of smooth, understated performances that define crooning, with Krall's soft, smoky voice perfectly suited to the romantic ballads and jazz standards she has made her own. Like Connick and Bublé, Krall has managed to keep the spirit of crooning alive, bringing the emotional depth and intimacy of the style to a new generation of listeners.

What's been particularly interesting about the crooning revival of the 1990s and 2000s is how it has managed to cross genres and find its way into all kinds of musical spaces. While Connick, Bublé, and Krall represent the more traditional side of crooning, the influence of the style can be heard in the work of many other modern artists as well. Singers like John Legend, with his soulful, romantic ballads, or even Lana Del Rey, with her nostalgic, cinematic sound, have tapped into the emotional sincerity and intimacy that are the hallmarks of crooning.

In the digital age, crooning has found a new home, not just in live performances or physical albums, but on streaming platforms and social media. Younger audiences, who might not have grown up listening to Sinatra or Bennett, have discovered crooning through platforms like Spotify and YouTube, where entire catalogues of classic crooner albums are just a click away. And, thanks to artists like Connick and Bublé, crooning has remained relevant, with modern-day crooners continuing to release albums and perform sold-out shows around the world.

For me, as a crooner, this revival has been incredibly exciting to witness. It's a reminder that, no matter how much music changes, there will always be a place for a voice that can tell a story, that can make you feel something real. Crooning, at its core, is about connection, it's about using your voice to create an emotional bond with the listener, to make them feel like they're part of the experience. That's something that will never go out of style.

Looking ahead, I have no doubt that crooning will continue to evolve and find its place in the modern music landscape. New artists will emerge, inspired by the greats of the past, and they will bring their own voices and stories to the tradition. And as long as there are listeners who crave that sense of intimacy and connection, crooning will never truly fade away. It's a timeless art, one that has been passed down from generation to generation, and it will continue to resonate with audiences for years to come.

CHAPTER 17: THE CRAFT OF CROONING: TECHNIQUE AND MASTERY

When people think about crooning, they often focus on the romance, the storytelling, and the emotional connection that the singer creates with the listener. But behind that smooth, effortless delivery is an immense amount of technical skill. Crooning may sound easy and natural, but it's an art form that requires a deep understanding of vocal technique, breath control, and microphone mastery. It's the subtle combination of these elements that makes crooning so unique, and so challenging to perfect.

One of the most important aspects of crooning is microphone technique. Unlike many other styles of singing, where vocal power and projection are key, crooning is all about intimacy. The microphone is your closest ally, it allows you to sing softly, to let the nuances of your voice come through without having to shout or strain. It's a tool that, when used properly, can turn even the quietest note into something rich and full of meaning.

I've always thought of the microphone as an extension of my voice. It's not just there to amplify sound, it's there to help shape the performance, to create the illusion that the singer is right there in the room with you, singing just for you. Crooners like Bing Crosby and Frank Sinatra understood this better than anyone. They knew how to use the microphone to their advantage, leaning into it for those soft, intimate moments and pulling back slightly when they needed to give the song a little more punch.

Microphone placement is crucial when it comes to crooning. The closer you are to the microphone, the more intimate the sound will be. This is perfect for ballads and softer songs where you want the listener to feel like you're speaking directly to them. But it's not just about singing quietly, it's about controlling the dynamics of your voice, knowing when to lean in and when to pull back to create contrast and emotion in the performance. Too much of either, and you risk losing the emotional depth of the song.

Breath control is another essential component of crooning. Because crooning often involves long, sustained notes and phrases, it's important to have strong breath support to keep the voice steady and controlled. This can be particularly challenging when singing softly, as it's easy to run out of breath or lose the tone if you're not properly supported. The key is to use your diaphragm, not your throat, to control the airflow, allowing you to maintain a smooth, even tone throughout the song.

One of the techniques I've found most useful in developing my breath control is the idea of "singing through the line." This means thinking about each phrase as one continuous idea, rather than chopping it up into individual words or notes. By focusing on the overall shape of the phrase, rather than each individual note, you can create a more fluid, natural sound. It also helps to prevent the voice from sounding too rigid or mechanical, which can easily happen if you're too focused on hitting every note perfectly.

Another important aspect of breath control in crooning is knowing when to breathe. Unlike in more operatic or belted styles of singing, where breaths can be taken more freely between phrases, crooning often requires the singer to hold back and make more strategic choices about where to breathe. The goal is to keep the phrases as smooth and connected as possible, so the listener isn't distracted by unnecessary breaks in the music. It's a delicate balance, and one that takes a lot of practice to perfect.

Phrasing is another key element that sets crooning apart from other styles of singing. Crooners are storytellers at heart, and phrasing is the tool they use to bring those stories to life. It's about more than just singing the notes on the page, it's about how you shape each word, how you choose to pause or stretch certain syllables, and how you use the rhythm of the song to guide the listener through the emotional arc of the lyrics.

Frank Sinatra was a master of phrasing, often described as "playing the words like an instrument." He had an incredible ability to make every line feel conversational, as though he was speaking directly to you, rather than singing to an audience. This is the essence of great crooning, it's not about performing for a crowd, but about creating a personal connection with each listener. Sinatra would often play with the timing of a phrase, holding back just enough to build tension before releasing it at exactly the right moment. It was an art form in itself, and it's one of the reasons why his performances still resonate so deeply with listeners today.

Timing, in general, is crucial in crooning. Many of the best crooners have a jazz background, and that's no coincidence. Jazz is all about rhythm and timing, and that sense of swing and syncopation is often what gives crooning its unique feel. Knowing when to come in just behind the beat, or when to linger on a note a little longer than expected, can make all the difference in a performance. It's what creates that sense of ease, that feeling that the singer is completely in control of the song, guiding the listener through the music with subtlety and grace.

For me, one of the most rewarding parts of being a crooner is mastering these small, technical details. On the surface, crooning might seem simple, it's just singing softly, right? But the more you dive into it, the more you realise how much nuance is involved. Every decision, from how close you stand to the microphone to where you choose to breathe, affects the overall feel of the performance. It's a constant balancing act between technical precision and emotional expression, and when it all comes together, it creates something magical.

But of course, all the technique in the world means nothing if you're not connecting with the song. At the heart of crooning is a deep emotional connection to the music. As a crooner, your job is to tell the story of the song, to inhabit the lyrics and make the listener feel what you're feeling. This is what separates great crooners from good ones, the ability to transcend the technical aspects of the performance and deliver something that feels real and personal.

For me, the best performances are the ones where I lose myself in the song, where I'm not thinking about microphone placement or breath control, but simply letting the music flow through me. It's about finding that balance between technique and emotion, where the two come together to create something that feels effortless, even though you know it took years of practice to get there.

Another essential aspect of crooning is tone. Crooners are known for their smooth, rich vocal tones, and developing that sound takes time and patience. Unlike belters or rock singers, who might rely on power or grit to convey emotion, crooners use a softer, more controlled tone to draw the listener in. The goal is to make the voice sound warm and inviting, like a conversation with an old friend.

Developing a consistent, warm tone requires a lot of vocal training. It's about learning how to use your voice in a way that minimises strain and maximises resonance. One of the techniques I use to achieve this is vocal placement, specifically, focusing the sound in the mask of the face (the area around the nose, cheeks, and forehead) rather than in the throat or chest. This allows for a more resonant sound that feels full without being overpowering.

One of the joys of crooning is that it allows for a wide range of vocal expression within a relatively small dynamic range. Unlike more dramatic styles of singing, crooning doesn't require huge jumps in volume or intensity. Instead, the magic comes from subtle changes in tone, phrasing, and dynamics. It's about finding the emotional core of a song and using your voice to express that emotion in the most sincere and personal way possible.

As a crooner, I've spent years honing these skills, always striving to improve my technique while staying true to the heart of the music. It's a never-ending journey, one that challenges me with every performance. But that's what makes crooning so special, it's not about showing off or impressing the audience. It's about creating a moment of connection, about using your voice to tell a story, and about inviting the listener to share in that story with you.

In the end, crooning is both an art and a craft. It requires technical mastery, but it also requires heart. And when those two elements come together, when the technique is so finely tuned that it disappears into the emotion of the performance, that's when the magic happens.

WAYNEDEVLINBCAA

CHAPTER 18: THE EMOTIONAL CORE OF CROONING

At the heart of crooning lies something much deeper than vocal technique or style, it's the raw emotion that pours through every note. What sets crooning apart from other forms of singing is the way it taps into the most human of experiences: love, longing, heartache, joy, and vulnerability. It's a style that doesn't rely on grand vocal theatrics to make an impact; instead, it uses subtlety, sincerity, and emotion to create a lasting connection with the audience.

For me, this emotional core is what drew me to crooning in the first place. I've always believed that music is about more than just entertainment, it's about connection. It's about using your voice to share something personal and real with the listener, to make them feel something that resonates on a deeper level. And crooning, with its intimate, conversational style, is perfectly suited to that kind of emotional storytelling.

When I think about the greatest crooners, people like Frank Sinatra, Nat King Cole, Tony Bennett, they all have one thing in common: they make you feel like you're not just listening to a song, but experiencing a moment of their lives. There's a sense of intimacy in the way they sing, as though they're opening a window into their hearts and inviting you in. Whether they're singing about the exhilaration of new love or the devastation of a broken heart, their voices carry a sincerity that cuts through all the noise and speaks directly to the listener's soul.

That's what makes crooning so powerful, it's not about impressing the audience with vocal gymnastics or dramatic flair. It's about finding the emotional truth of the song and communicating that truth in the simplest, most direct way possible. And because crooners sing softly, because they don't rely on power to get their point across, every little inflection, every breath, every pause becomes important. There's no room for hiding behind big gestures or showy techniques, the emotion has to come from a place of honesty.

Take Frank Sinatra, for example. He had an uncanny ability to make you believe every word he sang. When you listen to him sing One for My Baby (and One More for the Road), you can feel the weight of his sadness, the loneliness of sitting at the bar with a drink in his hand, reflecting on lost love. It's not just a song, it's a moment, a snapshot of a man's heart laid bare. Sinatra wasn't afraid to let his voice carry the weight of those emotions, and that's why his performances continue to resonate with listeners long after the song has ended.

But this emotional depth isn't just reserved for ballads or sad songs. Even in more upbeat numbers, crooners find a way to inject a sense of joy or longing that makes the performance feel real. Nat King Cole, for instance, could sing a song like L-O-V-E with such warmth and sincerity that it felt like he was singing just for you. There's a reason his music has been used in countless romantic moments, it's because his voice had a way of making you believe in the simple beauty of love. He didn't need to belt out the song or over-embellish it; he just let the words and the melody do the talking, allowing his voice to carry the joy and hope of the message.

When I step onto the stage as a crooner, my goal is always the same: to connect with the audience on an emotional level. Whether I'm singing to a room full of people or just one person in the crowd, I want to make them feel something real. That's why I always focus on the lyrics, on the story behind the song. Every song has a story to tell, and as a crooner, it's my job to bring that story to life, to give it meaning beyond the notes and chords. It's about putting yourself into the song, finding a way to relate to the emotions it's expressing, and then sharing that with the listener.

Of course, this isn't always easy. As performers, we all have days when we're not feeling our best, when it's hard to tap into that emotional core. But with crooning, you can't afford to phone it in. The audience will know if you're not fully present, if you're just going through the motions. Crooning demands that you be emotionally vulnerable, that you open yourself up to the song and to the audience. And while that can be challenging, it's also what makes crooning so rewarding. When you truly connect with the song, when you lose yourself in the music and allow the emotions to take over, the audience can feel it. It's those moments of pure emotion that leave a lasting impact.

I often think about how crooning, in its purest form, is like a conversation between the singer and the listener. It's not about performing for someone, it's about sharing something with them. That's why the best crooners don't just sing, they communicate. They use their voices to express emotions that words alone can't capture. Whether it's the soft sigh of a heartbroken lyric or the gentle lift of a hopeful refrain, every note is a piece of the conversation, a way of reaching out to the listener and saying, "I understand what you're feeling."

This is why crooning works so well with love songs. Love, in all its forms, romantic love, lost love, unrequited love, is at the core of so many crooner performances. And that's because crooning is about vulnerability, about allowing yourself to feel deeply and to express those feelings through your voice. Love songs, with their simple but profound messages, provide the perfect vehicle for that kind of emotional expression. Whether you're singing about the thrill of falling in love or the heartbreak of watching it slip away, there's an honesty in love songs that fits perfectly with the crooning style.

But crooning isn't just about love. It's about all the emotions that make us human, joy, sadness, hope, despair, longing. As crooners, we have the unique ability to tap into those emotions and share them with our audience in a way that feels personal and real. And in a world that can often feel disconnected and distant, that kind of emotional connection is more important than ever.

For me, some of the most powerful moments as a performer come when I can see that connection happening in real time. It's in the way someone's eyes light up during a particularly poignant lyric, or the way a couple leans into each other during a love song. It's in the quiet after the last note has been sung, when the audience is sitting in silence, absorbing what they've just heard. Those are the moments that make all the hard work worth it. That's when you know that you've done your job, that you've reached someone on a deeper level.

One of the reasons crooning has endured for so long, even through all the changes in popular music, is because it taps into something universal. No matter who you are or where you come from, you've experienced the emotions that crooners sing about. You've loved, you've lost, you've hoped, you've hurt. And when a crooner steps up to the microphone and sings about those things, it's like they're giving voice to your own experiences. That's the power of crooning, it makes the personal universal, and the universal personal.

As a crooner, I'm constantly working to improve my technique, to refine my craft. But at the end of the day, all the technique in the world won't matter if you're not connecting with the audience.

That's what crooning is really about—finding that emotional core and using your voice to express it in the most sincere, authentic way possible. It's about creating a moment that feels real, that lingers long after the song has ended.

In the end, crooning is more than just a style of singing, it's a way of communicating, a way of reaching out and making people feel something. It's an art form that requires not only skill but heart. And when those two things come together, when the technique and the emotion are perfectly balanced, that's when the magic happens. That's when a song becomes more than just a song, it becomes an experience, a memory, a feeling that stays with you long after the music has stopped.

CHAPTER 19: CROONING'S CULTURAL IMPACT: ELEGANCE, ROMANCE, AND COOL

While crooning is first and foremost a musical art form, its influence extends far beyond the songs themselves. Over the decades, crooners have become more than just singers, they've become cultural icons, symbols of elegance, romance, and a kind of effortless cool that resonates across generations. Their smooth voices, combined with their impeccable style and stage presence, made them not just stars of the music world but key figures in the broader cultural landscape.

In many ways, crooning helped define what it meant to be a modern gentleman in the mid-20th century. The classic image of a crooner, dressed in a sharp suit, standing under the spotlight, microphone in hand, became synonymous with sophistication, charm, and class. Men like Frank Sinatra and Dean Martin weren't just admired for their voices; they were admired for the way they carried themselves, the way they seemed to glide through life with an effortless cool that made everything look easy. And for many listeners, especially in the post-war era, crooners represented an ideal to aspire to, a way of being that combined grace, confidence, and emotional depth.

Frank Sinatra, perhaps more than any other crooner, embodied this cultural ideal. His voice was the soundtrack to countless romantic moments, but it was his persona that made him a cultural icon. Sinatra wasn't just a singer, he was the epitome of cool. He exuded confidence without arrogance, charm without effort. Whether he was performing on stage, acting in films, or simply being photographed out on the town, Sinatra's image was one of effortless sophistication. He made being a crooner seem not just like a job but a lifestyle, one that combined glamour, romance, and a kind of laid-back swagger that has rarely been matched.

Sinatra's influence extended beyond music into fashion, cinema, and even politics. His trademark fedora, impeccably tailored suits, and polished appearance set a standard for men's fashion that lasted for decades. Even today, when people think of classic men's style, Sinatra's image comes to mind. He understood the power of presentation, of creating a cohesive image that was as much a part of his appeal as his voice. And it wasn't just his look, his attitude, his way of being, became a template for what it meant to be cool in mid-20th century America.

Sinatra's relationship with his audience also reflected the power of crooning as a cultural force. He had the ability to make every listener feel like they were part of an exclusive club, a group of people who understood the finer things in life, good music, good company, and a glass of whiskey at the end of the day. This sense of intimacy, of creating a personal connection with his fans, is what made crooners like Sinatra so beloved. It wasn't just about the music, it was about the lifestyle, the world they created through their songs.

But it wasn't just Sinatra who became a cultural icon through crooning. Dean Martin, often considered the more laid-back counterpart to Sinatra's cool precision, brought a sense of humour and warmth to the crooner image. Martin's persona was that of the charming, easy-going entertainer, always ready with a joke or a smile. His voice, rich and smooth, combined with his playful on-stage banter, made him one of the most beloved entertainers of his era. He was the life of the party, the guy everyone wanted to have a drink with, and his relaxed, carefree style added a new dimension to the image of the crooner.

Dean Martin's variety show in the 1960s further cemented his status as a cultural icon. The Dean Martin Show wasn't just a showcase for his singing, it was a celebration of the crooner lifestyle, complete with casual performances, celebrity guests, and Martin's signature humour. The show was hugely popular, not just because of the music, but because of the atmosphere Martin created, a world where everyone was welcome, where the drinks were always flowing, and where the music was always smooth.

Tony Bennett, on the other hand, brought a different kind of elegance to the world of crooning. While Sinatra and Martin represented a kind of American cool, Bennett embodied a more refined, international sensibility. His voice, warm and full of emotion, was perfectly suited to the romantic ballads and jazz standards he became famous for. But beyond his voice, Bennett's career has been defined by his commitment to artistry and his refusal to compromise his musical integrity. He didn't chase trends or fads, he stayed true to the Great American Songbook, and in doing so, became a symbol of timelessness.

Bennett's long career, which has spanned more than seven decades, is a testament to the enduring power of crooning as an art form. Even as musical trends came and went, Bennett remained a constant, a reminder that there will always be an audience for music that speaks to the heart. His late-career resurgence, particularly through his collaborations with younger artists like Lady Gaga, has shown that crooning is not just a relic of the past, it's something that continues to resonate with new generations of listeners.

The cultural impact of crooning extends beyond the individual singers themselves. Crooners helped shape the way people thought about romance, about relationships, and about expressing emotion. In a time when masculinity was often associated with stoicism and emotional reserve, crooners gave men permission to be vulnerable, to sing about love and loss in a way that was sincere and heartfelt. They showed that it was possible to be both strong and sensitive, to embrace both the highs and lows of life with grace and dignity.

For women, too, crooning held a special appeal. Crooners sang about love in a way that felt personal, as though they were speaking directly to you. Their voices, soft and intimate, created a sense of closeness that made every song feel like a shared experience. It's no wonder that so many of the great love songs of the 20th century were written for crooners, their ability to convey deep emotion with such subtlety made them the perfect voices for expressing the complexities of the human heart.

But beyond romance, crooning also carried a sense of aspiration. The crooner lifestyle, the sharp suits, the glamorous nightclubs, the late-night drinks, was something to be admired, something to strive for. In a world that was rapidly changing, where technology and modernisation were transforming everyday life, crooners represented a link to a simpler, more elegant time. They were the soundtrack to people's dreams, to their hopes for a life filled with love, beauty, and sophistication.

Even today, the influence of crooning can be felt in popular culture. You see it in the enduring appeal of classic fashion, in the way young artists still look to Sinatra or Bennett as benchmarks of what it means to be a true performer. Crooning has also left its mark on cinema, with films like La La Land and The Great Gatsby drawing heavily from the aesthetic and emotional power of the crooner era. The timeless elegance of crooning has a way of creeping back into the cultural conversation, reminding us that some things never go out of style.

For me, as a crooner, I've always been aware of the cultural legacy that comes with the music. It's not just about singing a song, it's about carrying on a tradition, about embodying a certain ideal of elegance, romance, and emotional honesty. Every time I step onto the stage, I think about the greats who came before me, about the way they used their voices not just to entertain, but to connect, to create something lasting and meaningful.

Crooning may have started as a style of singing, but over the years, it has become so much more. It's a cultural touchstone, a symbol of a way of life that values beauty, grace, and emotional depth. And while the music world will continue to evolve, I have no doubt that the spirit of crooning will endure, quietly shaping the way we think about music, about love, and about what it means to truly connect with an audience.

CHAPTER 20: THE ART OF LIVE PERFORMANCE: CROONING IN THE MOMENT

There's something undeniably special about live performance. It's a moment where everything, the music, the audience, the performer, comes together in real time, creating a connection that can't be replicated in the studio. For crooners, live performance has always been at the heart of the art form. While recordings can capture the intimacy and emotion of a crooner's voice, there's nothing quite like being in the room when that voice fills the space, when the notes hang in the air and the audience holds its breath in anticipation.

For me, live performance is where the magic happens. As a crooner, stepping onto the stage isn't just about singing the songs, it's about creating an atmosphere, about inviting the audience into a world where emotion and melody reign supreme. It's about connecting with each person in the room, making them feel like they're part of something personal and intimate, even if they're sitting at the back of the theatre. That's the power of live performance, and it's something that every crooner, from Sinatra to Bennett, has understood.

One of the unique challenges of live performance, especially for a crooner, is maintaining that sense of intimacy, even in a large venue. Crooning is a style that was built for small, smoky clubs, where the singer could make eye contact with the audience, where every note could be delivered with the quiet sincerity that defines the genre. But over the years, crooners have performed in much larger spaces, concert halls, arenas, even stadiums. The challenge, then, is to make the audience feel like they're still in that small club, even if they're sitting in the nosebleed section.

This is where stage presence comes into play. Crooners are often described as being cool, effortless, in control, and that's exactly what the best live performances convey. It's about creating a sense of calm on stage, a feeling that you're completely at ease with the music, with the audience, and with the moment. When you're a crooner, the goal isn't to dazzle the audience with vocal acrobatics or high-energy choreography. It's about drawing them in, using your voice and your presence to make them feel like they're part of something special.

For me, one of the most important aspects of performing live is reading the room. Every audience is different, and part of the art of live performance is being able to adapt to the energy of the crowd. Sometimes, you're in front of an audience that's hanging on your every word, completely captivated by the music. Other times, you might have a crowd that's a little harder to engage, that needs to be coaxed into the moment. As a crooner, it's your job to find that connection, to figure out what the audience needs and to give it to them.

One of the techniques I've developed over the years is starting a performance with a slower, more intimate song. It helps to set the tone, to bring the audience into the world I'm creating. Crooning is about subtlety, about taking your time and letting the emotion build naturally. By starting with something soft and soulful, I can create a sense of intimacy right from the beginning, allowing the audience to settle into the performance and become more receptive to the music.

But of course, live performance isn't just about the slow ballads. Even in the most relaxed crooning sets, there's room for energy, for excitement, for moments that lift the crowd and get them moving. Songs like Fly Me to the Moon or Mack the Knife have an inherent swing to them, a rhythm that can fill the room with energy. The key is knowing how to balance those moments with the quieter, more introspective songs, so that the audience feels like they're on a journey with you, experiencing the full range of emotions that the music has to offer.

The pacing of a live performance is crucial for a crooner. Unlike rock concerts or pop shows, where the goal might be to keep the energy high throughout, crooning is about dynamics, about giving the audience moments to breathe, to reflect, and to feel. It's a delicate balance, too many slow songs, and the energy can dip; too many upbeat numbers, and you lose the emotional depth that crooning is known for. Finding that balance, creating a setlist that flows naturally from one emotion to the next, is one of the most rewarding parts of preparing for a live performance.

One of the great things about crooning is that it allows for spontaneity. Because the style is so conversational, so intimate, there's always room for improvisation in a live setting. Whether it's a small change in phrasing, a moment where you pause to interact with the audience, or even a surprise song choice, live performance gives you the freedom to respond to the moment. That's one of the things I love most about being a crooner, you're never locked into a rigid performance. You can let the music breathe, let the audience guide you, and adapt to the energy in the room.

Some of my most memorable performances have been the ones where something unexpected happened, where a song took on new meaning because of the way the audience responded, or where a moment of improvisation led to something beautiful and unplanned. That's the magic of live music, especially in crooning. You never know exactly how the night is going to unfold, but if you're open to the moment, it can lead to something truly special.

One of the greatest examples of a crooner who mastered the art of live performance was Frank Sinatra. Watching Sinatra on stage, you could see how he effortlessly controlled the room, how he used his voice and his charisma to create an atmosphere of cool sophistication. But beyond that, Sinatra had an incredible ability to connect with his audience in real time. He knew how to play to the crowd, how to make every person in the room feel like they were part of the show. Whether he was joking with the band, chatting with the audience, or delivering a heart-wrenching ballad, Sinatra was always in the moment, always aware of the energy in the room.

Sinatra also understood the importance of pacing in a live performance. His setlists were carefully curated to take the audience on a journey, moving from upbeat swing numbers to quiet, emotional ballads with ease. He knew when to bring the energy up and when to let it simmer, creating a performance that felt dynamic and alive. Even in the largest concert halls, Sinatra made you feel like you were right there with him, sharing in the moment.

Tony Bennett, too, is a master of live performance. Even well into his 80s and 90s, Bennett continued to perform with a level of grace and skill that many younger singers could only dream of. His live shows were a masterclass in how to create intimacy with an audience, even in a large venue. Bennett's voice, always warm and full of emotion, seemed to wrap around the room, drawing the audience into his world. And like Sinatra, Bennett knew how to balance the light and the dark, the joy and the sorrow, in his setlists, creating performances that left a lasting emotional impact.

For me, live performance is the ultimate test of a crooner's artistry. It's where all the technical skills, all the emotional depth, and all the years of practice come together in real time. There's no room for second takes, no chance to edit or polish the performance afterward. It's raw, it's real, and it's happening right in front of the audience. And that's what makes it so powerful. When you're up there, under the lights, with nothing but your voice and the music, it's just you and the audience. And in that moment, you have the opportunity to create something unforgettable.

I've learned over the years that no two performances are ever the same. Each show brings its own set of challenges and rewards, its own unique energy. But that's what makes live performance so exciting, there's always the potential for something magical to happen, something that can only be experienced in that moment, in that room, with that particular audience. It's a shared experience, one that leaves both the performer and the listener changed in some small way.

As a crooner, I take pride in the fact that live performance is at the heart of what I do. It's where the music comes alive, where the stories are told in real time, and where the connection between singer and audience is at its most powerful. It's a craft, a skill, and an art form that I continue to refine with every show. And no matter how many performances I give, that feeling of stepping onto the stage, of seeing the faces in the crowd and hearing the first note ring out, never gets old.

In the end, live performance is about creating a moment, about sharing something personal and real with the audience. It's about bringing the music to life in a way that recordings simply can't capture. And for me, as a crooner, that's the ultimate reward.

CHAPTER 21: CROONING'S INFLUENCE ON MODERN GENRES

It's easy to think of crooning as something that belongs to a bygone era, a relic of the golden age of radio and vinyl records. But the truth is that the essence of crooning, its emotional depth, its vocal subtlety, and its focus on intimacy, has had a lasting impact on modern music. From pop to indie, from jazz to R&B, you can hear echoes of the crooning tradition in many of today's most popular genres. Even in an age dominated by digital production and high-energy performances, the art of crooning continues to inspire and shape the way artists approach their craft.

One of the most noticeable ways crooning has influenced modern music is in the resurgence of the pop ballad. While pop music is often associated with catchy hooks and danceable beats, ballads have always held a special place in the genre, providing a space for artists to slow down, strip back the production, and focus on the emotional core of the song. Many of today's biggest pop stars, from Adele to Sam Smith, have embraced the ballad as a way to showcase their vocal abilities and connect with listeners on a deeper level. And in doing so, they're tapping into the same emotional sincerity that defined the classic crooners.

Take Adele, for instance. Songs like Someone Like You and When We Were Young are modern-day ballads that wouldn't feel out of place in a crooner's repertoire. Adele's voice, rich with emotion and vulnerability, is often compared to the great singers of the past, and it's no wonder, she sings with the kind of heart and soul that goes right to the listener's core. She doesn't need flashy production or over-the-top vocal runs to make an impact; instead, she relies on her ability to convey deep emotion through the simplicity of her voice. That's a hallmark of crooning, letting the emotion speak for itself.

Similarly, Sam Smith has often been described as a modern crooner, thanks to their smooth, controlled voice and their ability to sing about love and heartbreak with emotional precision. Songs like Stay With Me and Too Good at Goodbyes are steeped in the tradition of crooning, with their focus on romantic longing and emotional vulnerability. Smith, like the crooners before them, knows how to make a song feel personal and intimate, drawing the listener into their world with each note.

But it's not just pop ballads where you can hear the influence of crooning. Jazz, which has always been closely linked with crooning, continues to evolve, and many modern jazz vocalists are keeping the crooning tradition alive while pushing the boundaries of the genre. Artists like Norah Jones and Gregory Porter are perfect examples of how crooning can blend with contemporary jazz to create something new and exciting.

Norah Jones, with her soft, smoky voice, often channels the spirit of classic crooners like Billie Holiday and Peggy Lee. Her music, a blend of jazz, folk, and pop, has a laid-back intimacy that draws the listener in. Songs like Don't Know Why and Come Away With Me have that same emotional depth and understated elegance that define crooning, even though they exist in a more contemporary musical landscape. Jones doesn't just sing, she tells stories, using her voice to convey the quiet moments of life, much like the crooners who came before her.

Gregory Porter, on the other hand, has a more traditional jazz background, but his voice carries the warmth and richness of a classic crooner. Songs like Hey Laura and Liquid Spirit showcase his ability to blend jazz with soul, but it's his emotional delivery that sets him apart. Porter sings with a sincerity and openness that's reminiscent of the great crooners, and his live performances, where he connects deeply with his audience, are a testament to the enduring power of the crooning tradition.

Even in indie music, where experimentation and boundary-pushing are the norm, you can hear the subtle influence of crooning. Artists like Father John Misty and Alex Turner of Arctic Monkeys have incorporated elements of crooning into their music, using their voices to create a sense of intimacy and emotional depth in their performances. Father John Misty, for instance, often blends ironic detachment with moments of genuine vulnerability, and his vocal delivery is smooth, controlled, and full of emotional nuance. On albums like I Love You, Honeybear, you can hear the influence of the classic crooners in the way he shapes his phrases and uses his voice to tell a story.

Alex Turner, particularly on Arctic Monkeys' Tranquility Base Hotel & Casino, channels a lounge-singer vibe that harks back to the crooners of the 1950s and 1960s. His vocal delivery on songs like Four Out of Five and The Ultracheese has a kind of laid-back cool that feels very much in line with the crooning tradition. Turner's ability to blend modern indie rock with a crooner's sense of timing and phrasing is a testament to the enduring appeal of the style.

Another area where crooning's influence can be felt is in the world of R&B. Crooning and R&B have always had a close relationship, with both genres rooted in emotional expression and vocal nuance. Modern R&B singers like John Legend and Miguel often incorporate elements of crooning into their performances, using their voices to create moments of intimacy and connection with the listener.

John Legend, in particular, has a vocal style that feels steeped in the crooning tradition. His voice, warm and full of emotion, is perfectly suited to the romantic ballads he's known for. Songs like All of Me and Ordinary People are modern R&B tracks, but they carry the same emotional weight and sincerity as a classic crooner ballad. Legend's ability to make every note feel personal and heartfelt is what sets him apart, and it's a direct continuation of the crooning tradition.

Miguel, on the other hand, brings a more experimental approach to his music, blending R&B with rock, funk, and electronic elements. But at the core of his sound is his voice, which has a smoothness and control that wouldn't feel out of place in the world of crooning. Songs like Adorn and Coffee showcase his ability to bring emotional depth to his performances, using his voice to create a sense of intimacy and connection with the listener.

Even in the world of hip-hop, where vocals are often more rhythmic and percussive, you can hear the influence of crooning in the way some artists approach melody and emotional storytelling. Artists like Drake and The Weeknd have often been described as "modern crooners" thanks to their use of melody and their focus on themes of love, heartbreak, and vulnerability. While their music may be far removed from the classic crooners of the past, there's a direct line that connects their emotional delivery to the tradition of crooning.

Drake, with his often melancholy and introspective lyrics, has a vocal delivery that's smooth and melodic, even when he's rapping. Songs like Hold On, We're Going Home and Marvins

Room showcase his ability to blend hip-hop with R&B, creating tracks that feel intimate and emotionally raw. While Drake may not be a crooner in the traditional sense, his focus on emotional storytelling and his use of melody in his vocals place him firmly in the lineage of artists who use their voices to connect with listeners on a deeper level.

The Weeknd, with his ethereal voice and often dark, brooding lyrics, has also been described as a modern-day crooner. His songs, which often explore themes of love, lust, and heartbreak, are steeped in emotion, and his vocal delivery, smooth, controlled, and full of nuance, carries a sense of intimacy that's reminiscent of the great crooners. Tracks like Earned It and Call Out My Name showcase his ability to create a mood, to use his voice to draw the listener into his world in much the same way that Sinatra or Bennett might have done decades earlier.

What's clear from all of this is that crooning, far from being a relic of the past, is still very much alive in modern music. Whether it's through the ballads of pop stars like Adele and Sam Smith, the jazz-inflected performances of artists like Gregory Porter and Norah Jones, or the emotional storytelling of R&B and hip-hop artists like John Legend and The Weeknd, the influence of crooning can be heard across a wide range of genres. The emotional depth, vocal control, and focus on intimacy that define crooning have proven to be timeless, qualities that continue to resonate with both artists and listeners today.

As a crooner myself, it's exciting to see how the style continues to evolve and influence new generations of musicians. The essence of crooning, the ability to connect with an audience through emotion and storytelling, remains as relevant as ever, even as the musical landscape changes. It's a reminder that no matter how much music evolves, there will always be a place for a voice that can make you feel something real.

CHAPTER 22: THE TIMELESS LEGACY OF TONY BENNETT

When I think about the lasting legacy of crooning, there is no name more synonymous with the art form than Tony Bennett. Over the course of his extraordinary career, Tony Bennett became more than just a crooner, he became an icon, a living testament to the power of music to transcend time, generations, and trends. What makes Tony's legacy so remarkable is not just the longevity of his career, but the way he consistently stayed true to himself and the music he loved, even as the world around him changed.

Tony Bennett's story is one of resilience, passion, and unwavering dedication to his craft. Born Anthony Benedetto in 1926 in Astoria, Queens, Tony came from humble beginnings. His love for music was evident from an early age, and after serving in World War II, he returned to pursue a career as a singer. It didn't take long for his talent to be recognised, and by the 1950s, Bennett had become one of the most beloved crooners in the country, with hits like Because of You and Rags to Riches cementing his place in the American music scene.

But as musical tastes shifted in the 1960s and 1970s, Tony

Bennett, like many of his contemporaries, found himself facing new challenges. Rock and roll had taken over the charts, and the intimate, romantic style of crooning seemed to be falling out of favour with the younger generation. For many crooners, this shift marked the beginning of the end of their careers. But not for Tony Bennett.

Rather than trying to reinvent himself to fit the trends of the day, Bennett made a conscious decision to stay true to the music that had always defined him. He returned to his roots in jazz and the Great American Songbook, embracing the timeless songs that had shaped his career. This commitment to authenticity is what set Bennett apart. While other artists struggled to adapt to the changing musical landscape, Bennett remained a steadfast ambassador for the classics, and in doing so, he kept the tradition of crooning alive.

What's truly remarkable about Tony Bennett is the way he was able to connect with new generations of listeners, even as he stayed firmly rooted in the music of the past. In the 1990s, Bennett experienced an unexpected resurgence in popularity, thanks in part to his willingness to embrace new mediums and platforms. His appearance on MTV's Unplugged in 1994 introduced him to a younger audience, and the resulting album, Tony Bennett: MTV Unplugged, won him two Grammy Awards, including Album of the Year. It was a reminder that great music, delivered with heart and sincerity, never goes out of style.

But Bennett's resurgence wasn't just about adapting to new platforms, it was about his ability to forge genuine connections with listeners of all ages. There was a warmth and humility to Tony Bennett that resonated deeply with audiences. He wasn't just a singer, he was a storyteller, a performer who made you feel like you were the only person in the room, even if you were sitting in the back of a packed concert hall. That's the magic of Tony Bennett, and it's why his music continues to resonate with people of all generations.

One of the key moments in Tony Bennett's late-career resurgence came with his series of duets albums, where he collaborated with artists from a wide range of genres and backgrounds. Albums like Duets: An American Classic and Duets II featured Bennett singing alongside everyone from Barbra Streisand to Lady Gaga, and they showcased his incredible versatility as a performer. Whether he was singing with fellow legends like Stevie Wonder or collaborating with younger artists like John Mayer and Amy Winehouse, Bennett's voice remained as smooth, warm, and engaging as ever.

What was so impressive about these duets albums was the way Bennett was able to bridge the gap between generations. He wasn't just paying lip service to the younger artists he collaborated with, he was genuinely engaging with them, finding common ground in the music and creating performances that felt fresh and exciting. His collaboration with Lady Gaga, in particular, highlighted this ability. Their 2014 album Cheek to Cheek was a critical and commercial success, and it introduced Bennett's music to an entirely new generation of fans. The chemistry between the two was undeniable, and it was clear that Gaga had a deep respect for Bennett and the music he represented.

In many ways, Cheek to Cheek was a perfect encapsulation of what Tony Bennett's legacy is all about. Here was an artist who had been performing for more than six decades, still at the top of his game, still finding new ways to connect with audiences and share his love for the Great American Songbook. The album wasn't just a celebration of Bennett's career, it was a reminder that this music, these songs, are timeless. And Tony Bennett, with his incredible voice and his unwavering passion for the music, was the perfect ambassador for that timelessness.

But Tony Bennett's legacy isn't just about his music, it's about the way he lived his life. Throughout his career, Bennett remained humble, gracious, and deeply committed to using his platform for good. He was a lifelong advocate for civil rights, and his involvement in the civil rights movement of the 1960s, particularly his participation in the Selma to Montgomery marches alongside Martin Luther King Jr., spoke to his belief in equality and justice for all. Bennett also founded the Frank Sinatra School of the Arts in Queens, New York, as a way to give back to the community and support the next generation of artists.

Tony's commitment to social causes, combined with his dedication to his craft, made him not just a great artist, but a great human being. He was a man who never lost sight of what was truly important, connecting with people, sharing his love of music, and making a positive impact on the world. That's the legacy he leaves behind, and it's one that will continue to inspire generations of artists and listeners alike.

For me, Tony Bennett represents everything that's beautiful about crooning. His voice, always warm and full of heart, is a reminder that music is about connection, it's about using your voice to share something real, something that speaks to the human experience. And even as musical trends come and go, that core truth remains the same. Tony Bennett's career is proof of that. He showed us all that if you stay true to yourself, if you sing from the heart, your music will endure.

As I reflect on my own connection to Tony Bennett, I'm reminded of the profound impact he's had on my life as a crooner. Meeting him, receiving his support for my fundraiser, and hearing his words of encouragement were all moments that reaffirmed my belief in the power of music to bring people together. Tony Bennett's influence on me goes far beyond his voice, it's about the way he lived his life, the way he carried himself with grace and dignity, and the way he never stopped believing in the importance of music as a force for good.

Tony Bennett's legacy will live on, not just in his recordings, but in the countless lives he touched throughout his career. His music will continue to inspire new generations of singers and listeners, reminding us all that crooning is more than just a style of singing, it's a way of connecting with the world, one song at a time.

CHAPTER 23: CROONING IN THE DIGITAL AGE

As the world of music has evolved, so too has the way crooners reach their audiences. The rise of the digital age has transformed the music industry in ways that were unimaginable just a few decades ago. Streaming platforms, social media, and digital recording technology have revolutionised how music is created, shared, and consumed, and crooning, while rooted in tradition, has found new life in this ever-changing landscape.

At first glance, it might seem like crooning, with its emphasis on intimacy and emotional connection, would struggle to find a place in the fast-paced world of digital music. After all, crooning was born in a time when radio, vinyl records, and live performances were the primary ways people experienced music. The warmth of a crooner's voice seemed perfectly suited to the crackle of a vinyl record or the low hum of a live performance in a small, dimly lit club. But as technology has advanced, crooning has shown that it can adapt and thrive in the digital age.

One of the biggest changes brought about by the digital revolution is the way music is distributed. Streaming platforms like Spotify,

Apple Music, and YouTube have made it easier than ever for artists to share their music with the world. In the past, crooners like Frank Sinatra or Tony Bennett would rely on record labels, radio stations, and live performances to build their careers. But today, a singer can upload their music to a streaming platform and reach millions of listeners around the globe in an instant.

This has been a game-changer for both established crooners and up-and-coming artists. For established artists, streaming platforms have allowed their music to reach new audiences. Tony Bennett, for example, saw a resurgence in his popularity with younger listeners thanks in part to the availability of his music on streaming services. Younger generations, who may not have grown up listening to Bennett on the radio or on vinyl, were able to discover his timeless voice through digital platforms, introducing a whole new audience to the art of crooning.

For newer crooners, the digital age has provided opportunities that were previously unimaginable. Singers no longer need to rely on traditional gatekeepers like record labels or radio stations to get their music heard. With a well-produced track and a savvy social media strategy, an independent crooner can build a global fanbase from their living room. Artists like Michael Bublé, who came onto the scene just as the digital revolution was taking off, have been able to leverage these platforms to reach a worldwide audience, blending the classic crooning sound with modern marketing techniques.

Social media, in particular, has become a powerful tool for crooners to connect with their fans in new and meaningful ways. Platforms like Instagram, Twitter, and TikTok allow artists to share their music, their lives, and their personalities with their audience in real-time. For crooners, who have always relied on intimacy and connection as part of their appeal, social media offers a way to deepen that connection beyond the stage or the recording studio.

One of the most striking examples of this is how crooners have used social media to keep the Great American Songbook alive. While pop and hip-hop may dominate the charts, there is still a large and dedicated audience for the classic standards. Crooners like Michael Bublé, Diana Krall, and even Tony Bennett have used social media to share their love for these timeless songs, posting videos of live performances, sharing behind-the-scenes glimpses into the recording process, and engaging with fans who share their passion for the music.

Even more exciting is the way social media has allowed fans to interact with their favourite crooners in ways that would have been impossible in the past. In the era of Sinatra and Crosby, fans could listen to their records, attend their concerts, or send them fan mail. Today, a fan can comment on a post, send a message, or even have their favourite crooner respond directly to them. This level of interaction has helped to build a sense of community among fans, making the connection between artist and listener even more personal.

Another important aspect of the digital age is the rise of collaboration across genres and platforms. The ease with which artists can now record and share music has opened the door for collaborations that might have been difficult or even impossible in the past. Tony Bennett's duets with Lady Gaga, for example, were made possible not only by their mutual respect for each other's talents but by the technology that allowed them to bring their voices together in new and innovative ways.

This kind of cross-generational collaboration has helped keep crooning relevant in the modern music scene. Younger artists, who may not have grown up with crooners as their primary musical influence, are now discovering the beauty of the genre and incorporating its elements into their own work. And for older artists, these collaborations offer a way to stay connected with contemporary audiences while still staying true to their roots.

In many ways, the digital age has allowed crooning to reach new heights. While the genre will always be associated with the golden age of radio and vinyl, it has found a new home in the world of digital streaming and social media. Artists can now reach more people than ever before, sharing their music with a global audience and introducing new generations to the beauty and emotion of crooning.

But while technology has opened up new possibilities for crooners, it has also presented new challenges. In an age where listeners are bombarded with an endless stream of content, from TikTok videos to viral memes, it can be difficult to capture and hold their attention. Crooning, with its emphasis on subtlety, emotional depth, and nuance, can sometimes feel out of step with the fast-paced, attention-grabbing world of modern media.

However, I believe this is where crooning's greatest strength lies. In a world of constant noise and distraction, the quiet, heartfelt delivery of a crooner's voice offers a welcome reprieve. It's an invitation to slow down, to listen closely, and to feel something real. And for listeners who crave that kind of emotional connection, crooning will always have a place, no matter how much the world of music changes.

For me, the digital age has been both a challenge and an opportunity. As a crooner, I've had to adapt to new ways of reaching my audience, learning how to navigate social media and streaming platforms while staying true to the heart of my music. But I've also been able to connect with listeners in ways that would have been impossible even a few decades ago. Whether it's through a live-streamed concert, a social media post, or a new recording shared online, the digital world has allowed me to reach more people than ever before, and for that, I'm deeply grateful.

As I look to the future, I'm excited about the possibilities that the digital age holds for crooning. While the tools and platforms may change, the essence of the genre, the emotional connection, the intimacy, the storytelling, will always remain the same. And as long as there are listeners who crave that kind of connection, crooning will continue to thrive, finding new ways to adapt and evolve in a rapidly changing world.

CHAPTER 24: THE FUTURE OF CROONING: CARRYING THE TRADITION FORWARD

As I reflect on the long and storied history of crooning, I can't help but think about what the future holds for this art form. Crooning has endured through decades of changing musical landscapes, from the heyday of radio and big bands to the digital revolution of streaming and social media. It's a testament to the timeless appeal of crooning that it has managed to survive, and thrive, despite so many shifts in the industry. But what's even more exciting is the potential for crooning to continue evolving, to be embraced by new generations of singers and listeners alike.

At its core, crooning has always been about connection, about using the voice to create an emotional bond between the singer and the listener. That's why it has resonated so deeply with audiences over the years, and why I believe it will continue to do so for years to come. While musical trends may come and go, the desire for genuine emotional connection is something that will never fade. And crooning, with its emphasis on intimacy, storytelling, and sincerity, is uniquely suited to fulfilling that desire.

One of the most encouraging signs for the future of crooning is the way young artists are beginning to rediscover and reinterpret the genre. Singers like Michael Bublé and Norah Jones have already shown that there is a place for crooning in the modern music landscape, and their success has paved the way for even more artists to explore the style. But what's particularly exciting is the way these younger crooners are finding new ways to blend the classic elements of crooning with contemporary sounds, creating something that feels fresh while still staying true to the tradition.

Take Michael Bublé, for example. His music is deeply rooted in the crooning tradition, with its lush orchestral arrangements and romantic ballads. But he has also embraced elements of modern pop and jazz, creating a sound that feels both timeless and relevant to today's listeners. Bublé has successfully bridged the gap between generations, introducing younger audiences to the classic standards while also keeping his music fresh and contemporary.

What Bublé, and other modern crooners, have done so well is show that crooning doesn't have to be stuck in the past. While the Great American Songbook will always be an essential part of the crooning repertoire, there's room for new songs, new stories, and new ways of interpreting the genre. That's what will keep crooning alive and thriving in the years to come, the ability to adapt and evolve while staying true to the heart of the music.

And it's not just established artists who are carrying the torch for crooning. Thanks to the digital age, there are countless emerging singers who are discovering the beauty of the crooning style and bringing it into their own music. Platforms like YouTube, SoundCloud, and TikTok have made it easier than ever for young artists to share their music with the world, and many of them are turning to the classic crooner sound as a way to stand out in a crowded market.

What's particularly interesting is the way these younger crooners are blending genres and influences to create something entirely new. Some are fusing crooning with elements of R&B, indie, and even hip-hop, creating a sound that feels distinctly modern while still retaining the emotional depth and intimacy that defines crooning. It's a reminder that crooning is not just a relic of the past, it's a living, breathing art form that can be adapted to fit any musical context.

In many ways, this blending of genres is a natural evolution for crooning. After all, crooning itself was born out of a fusion of styles, combining elements of jazz, pop, and big band music to create something new and exciting. Today's young crooners are simply continuing that tradition, using the tools and influences of their time to create something that feels both fresh and familiar.

Another exciting development for the future of crooning is the increasing diversity of voices in the genre. While crooning has traditionally been associated with a certain type of male singer, smooth, suave, and effortlessly cool, today's crooners come from all walks of life, and they're bringing their own unique perspectives to the music. Female crooners like Diana Krall and Norah Jones have already shown that women can be just as effective in the genre as their male counterparts, and I believe we'll see even more diversity in the years to come.

This diversity extends not just to gender, but to musical background and cultural influences as well. Modern crooning is no longer confined to the world of jazz or the Great American Songbook. It's being embraced by artists from a wide range of genres and cultures, each bringing their own voice and experience to the music. This is an exciting development, as it ensures that crooning will continue to evolve and remain relevant in an increasingly globalised and interconnected world.

One of the keys to crooning's future success will be its ability to connect with younger audiences. While the classic crooners of the past still have a devoted following, it's important that new generations of listeners discover the beauty and power of the genre. This is where technology and social media will play a crucial role. Younger listeners are discovering music in different ways than previous generations, often through streaming platforms and social media rather than traditional radio or record stores. For crooning to remain relevant, it needs to be accessible to these younger audiences, and that means embracing the digital platforms where they spend their time.

But while technology can help crooning reach new audiences, the heart of the genre will always remain the same. Crooning is about more than just the songs, it's about the connection between the singer and the listener. It's about using the voice to tell a story, to convey an emotion, to make the listener feel something real. As long as crooners continue to prioritise that connection, the genre will continue to resonate with listeners, no matter how much the world around it changes.

As I think about my own role in the future of crooning, I'm filled with a sense of both responsibility and excitement. I feel a deep connection to the crooners who came before me, to the voices that have shaped my understanding of music and performance. But I'm also excited about the ways crooning can continue to evolve, about the new stories that can be told through this timeless style of singing. I'm committed to carrying the tradition forward, not just by honouring the past, but by embracing the future and finding new ways to keep crooning alive for the next generation.

Crooning, at its best, is an art form that transcends time. It speaks to something universal in the human experience, the desire for connection, for love, for meaning. And as long as there are singers who understand that, and listeners who crave it, crooning will never truly fade away. It will continue to evolve, to adapt, and to find its place in whatever new world we find ourselves in.

So, as we look to the future, I have no doubt that crooning will continue to thrive. It may look different than it did in the days of Sinatra or Bennett, but its essence will remain the same. It will always be about the voice, about the emotion, about the connection. And as long as we hold onto that, crooning will continue to captivate and inspire listeners for generations to come.

CHAPTER 25: CROONING'S ENDURING LEGACY

As we come to the end of this journey through the world of crooning, it's clear that this art form, born in the early 20th century, has left an indelible mark on music and culture. From the moment the microphone and radio brought crooners into the homes of listeners, their voices have been shaping the emotional landscape of generations. Crooning has transcended its origins in jazz and big band music to become a universal language of emotion, and its influence continues to resonate in music today.

What makes crooning so enduring is its timeless appeal. The smooth, intimate vocal style that defines crooning is something that cuts through the noise of trends and fads. Whether it's Frank Sinatra's effortless charm, Nat King Cole's warm sincerity, or Tony Bennett's ageless grace, crooners have always been able to connect with their audiences in a way that feels personal, even when heard through the static of a radio or the clarity of a streaming platform. Their voices carry a kind of emotional truth that transcends time and place.

The world of crooning has evolved over the years, but its essence remains unchanged. At its heart, crooning is about emotional connection. It's about taking the listener on a journey, whether that journey is one of love, heartbreak, hope, or nostalgia. The greatest crooners have always understood that it's not just about the notes you sing, it's about the feeling behind those notes, the story you're telling, and the way you make the listener feel. And that's something that will never go out of style.

One of the most remarkable aspects of crooning's legacy is how it has adapted to changing times without losing its core. The rise of rock and roll, disco, electronic music, and hip-hop may have shifted the spotlight away from crooning at various points, but it has never disappeared. Instead, crooning has quietly maintained its place in the musical world, always ready to re-emerge when the time is right. Artists like Michael Bublé, Norah Jones, Diana Krall, and Harry Connick Jr. have shown that crooning can be as relevant today as it was in the mid-20th century, and their success speaks to the enduring power of this vocal style.

For me, as a crooner, the legacy of those who came before me is something I carry with me every time I step onto the stage. When I sing, I'm not just performing a song, I'm continuing a tradition that has been passed down from generation to generation, from Bing Crosby to Tony Bennett, from Nat King Cole to Frank Sinatra. It's a tradition that values emotion over spectacle, sincerity over showmanship, and storytelling over simple entertainment. And that's what makes it so special.

I've had the privilege of learning from the greats, of studying their voices, their phrasing, their ability to connect with an audience. But I've also had the privilege of bringing my own voice, my own story, to the world of crooning. That's the beauty of this art form, it's a living, breathing tradition that allows each singer to put their own stamp on it, while still staying true to its core principles. Whether I'm singing a classic standard or a more contemporary song, I'm always thinking about how to make the music my own, how to bring something new to the conversation while honouring the legacy of those who came before me.

And that's where the future of crooning lies, in the ability to evolve, to adapt, and to remain relevant without losing sight of what makes it so special. As we look ahead, I have no doubt that new generations of singers will continue to find inspiration in the crooners of the past, just as I have. They'll bring their own voices, their own stories, and their own interpretations to the music, and in doing so, they'll keep the tradition alive.

The digital age has opened up new opportunities for crooners to connect with audiences in ways that were once unimaginable. Social media, streaming platforms, and digital recording technology have made it easier than ever for singers to share their music with the world, and crooning is no exception. But while the tools may have changed, the essence of crooning remains the same. It's about connection, about using your voice to create an emotional bond with the listener. And as long as crooners continue to prioritise that connection, the art form will continue to thrive.

But crooning's legacy isn't just about music, it's about culture. Crooners have always been more than just singers. They've been icons of style, grace, and elegance, representing a certain way of being that transcends the music itself. From Frank Sinatra's signature fedora to Tony Bennett's timeless tuxedo, crooners have always embodied a kind of effortless sophistication that has made them cultural figures in their own right. Their influence can be seen not just in music, but in fashion, film, and even the way we think about romance and relationships.

Crooners have given us the soundtrack to some of the most important moments in our lives, falling in love, experiencing heartbreak, dreaming of the future, reflecting on the past. Their voices have been there in the background, quietly guiding us through the highs and lows of life. And that's perhaps the greatest legacy of all, that crooning, with its emphasis on intimacy and emotion, has become a part of the fabric of our shared human experience.

As I look back on my own journey as a crooner, I'm filled with a sense of gratitude. Gratitude for the singers who inspired me, for the audiences who have listened to my voice, and for the music that has been such an important part of my life. Crooning has given me a way to connect with people, to share my emotions, and to be a part of something much larger than myself. And for that, I will always be thankful.

But more than that, I'm excited for the future of crooning. I believe that as long as there are singers who are willing to put their heart and soul into their music, crooning will continue to evolve, to adapt, and to inspire new generations of listeners. It's a timeless art form, one that speaks to something deep within us, and I have no doubt that it will continue to do so for years to come.

So as we close this chapter on the history and legacy of crooning, I invite you to keep listening, keep feeling, and keep connecting with the music. Whether it's a classic standard from the golden age of crooning or a new interpretation from a modern-day singer, the power of a great voice, telling a great story, will always have the ability to move us. And that, in the end, is what crooning is all about.

EPILOGUE

As I reflect on the journey through the history and evolution of crooning, I am reminded of its remarkable ability to endure across generations, cultures, and musical trends. At its core, crooning has always been about connection, between the singer and the listener, between the past and the present. It's a tradition that, no matter how much the world changes, continues to resonate deeply with audiences who crave sincerity, emotion, and intimacy in music.

For me, the legacy of Tony Bennett has been a constant source of inspiration, both in my career as a crooner and in my personal life. Tony was not just a brilliant artist, he was a gentleman, a role model, and a testament to the power of staying true to one's craft. His voice, which carried the weight of decades of storytelling, will continue to echo through time, a reminder that music can bridge the gap between generations, bringing people together through a shared love for timeless songs.

As we move forward, the art of crooning will no doubt continue to evolve. New voices will emerge, bringing their own interpretations and innovations to the tradition, while still holding on to the emotional depth and warmth that defines the genre. It is my hope that this book has not only given you an insight into the history and influence of crooning but also helped to deepen your appreciation for the voices that have shaped it, from the early pioneers to the modern-day legends.

For those of us who continue to carry the torch of crooning, whether on stage, in the studio, or simply in our hearts, we do so with a deep respect for the tradition that came before us and a hopeful eye toward the future. Crooning may have been born in the early days of radio and vinyl, but its spirit remains alive and well in the digital age, where the desire for meaningful, emotional music is stronger than ever.

Tony Bennett once said, "Life is a gift and I don't intend on wasting it," and in many ways, that sentiment encapsulates the heart of crooning. Each song, each performance, is a gift, a moment of connection, a shared experience. As I continue to sing, inspired by the voices of those who came before me, I am reminded of the beauty of that gift and the responsibility we have to keep it alive.

Thank you for joining me on this journey through the art of crooning. The voices may change, the songs may evolve, but the heart of crooning, the ability to make us feel deeply, to remind us of the beauty of life and love, will never fade. And for that, we will always be grateful.

— Wayne

AFTERWORD

As this book comes to a close, I find myself reflecting on the incredible journey that crooning has taken me on, not only through the exploration of its history and great figures but through my own personal experiences as a crooner. What started as an admiration for the great voices of the past, like Frank Sinatra and Tony Bennett, has become an integral part of who I am. Crooning is more than just a style of singing, it's a way of connecting, of sharing emotions, and of creating moments that resonate deeply with listeners.

Writing this book has allowed me to dive deeply into the origins and legacy of crooning. Along the way, I've been reminded that music, at its best, transcends time and trends. The timeless appeal of crooning lies in its emotional core, the way it draws the listener in, as if the singer is speaking directly to their heart. Through decades of change in the music industry, crooning has remained a beacon of sincerity and storytelling.

I've also been reminded of the profound impact that Tony Bennett has had, not only on the world of crooning but on my own life. Meeting Tony, receiving his words of encouragement, and being inspired by his resilience and dedication to his craft are moments I will carry with me always. He was more than just a singer, he was an ambassador of the values that crooning represents: integrity, grace, and a love for music that is pure and unwavering.

As we look to the future, I am filled with optimism for the art of crooning. New generations of artists are taking up the mantle, blending the classic sounds of the Great American Songbook with their own unique styles. The digital age has brought crooning to new audiences, and while the way we listen to music may have changed, the emotional connection that crooning offers will always be its greatest strength.

I hope that this book has given you a greater understanding of the rich history of crooning and the incredible voices that have defined it. But more than that, I hope it has inspired you to continue exploring this beautiful tradition, to seek out the voices that move you, and to appreciate the artistry that goes into every note, every phrase, and every story told through song.

For me, the journey of crooning is ongoing. Every performance is a new opportunity to connect, to create, and to honour the greats who came before me. And, in the spirit of Tony Bennett, I'll continue to sing for as long as my voice will allow, sharing the gift of music with those who are willing to listen.

Thank you for joining me on this journey.

— Wayne

Cystic Fibrosis a lifelong challenge
BRING HOPE
neu ven
UNITED CARGO
SENATOR INTERNATIONAL
PHMG/ FOUNDATION
ENTERTAINMENT TODAY
BENTLEY
HRIF

ACKNOWLEDGEMENT

Writing this book has been a deeply personal and rewarding journey, and I owe a great deal of thanks to the people who have supported and inspired me along the way.

First and foremost, I want to express my heartfelt gratitude to Tony Bennett, whose music and legacy have been the foundation of this book. His voice has been a guiding light in my career, and his kindness and encouragement have meant more to me than words can express. This book is, in many ways, a tribute to the impact he has had on my life and the world of music.

To my wonderful wife, Val, who has been by my side through every step of this journey. Your love, support, and belief in me have been my constant source of strength. From helping to arrange my meeting with Tony Bennett to standing by me during my fundraising marathon for Alzheimer's, you've been my rock in both life and music.

Thank you to my family and friends who have always been my biggest fans. Your support has carried me through countless performances, and your encouragement has pushed me to continue pursuing my passion for music.

I would also like to thank my mentors and musical influences, both those I've met and those I've admired from afar. Your guidance, advice, and wisdom have shaped me into the artist I am today.

A special thanks to the Manchester community, especially in Trafford and my home town of Urmston, and all those who have supported my performances and charity efforts over the years. Your enthusiasm and love for music have fueled my dedication to this craft.

To the Alzheimer's Society, for their tireless work in supporting those affected by this disease and for allowing me the opportunity to contribute through my music in Tony Bennett's honour.

Lastly, thank you to my readers. Without you, this book would not have been possible. I hope it serves as a testament to the enduring power of music, the legacy of crooning, and the timeless influence of Tony Bennett.

With sincere gratitude,

Wayne

ABOUT THE AUTHOR

Wayne Devlin Bcaa

Wayne Devlin is an award-winning jazz and swing vocalist from Manchester, UK, widely recognised as one of the finest crooners in the UK for his heartfelt renditions of the Great American Songbook. With a voice often compared to the great crooners like Frank Sinatra and Tony Bennett, Wayne has performed internationally, gracing stages from Las Vegas' Flamingo and Golden Nugget Casinos to venues in New York. His signature Rat Pack style has made him a go-to performer for celebrities such as Ian McShane, Denise Welch, Tyson Fury and Kym Marsh.

Wayne's love for the classics has not only fueled his successful music career but also led him to raise significant amounts for charity. He has raised over £750,000 for various charitable causes through performances and fundraising efforts, including his widely publicised 24-hour "swing-a-thon" in honour of Tony Bennett to support the Alzheimer's Society. His dedication to community service earned him the prestigious British Citizen Award (BCAa) for Services to the Arts, The Prime Minister's Points of Light Award and invites to 10 Downing Street and Buckingham Palace.

Beyond his vocal achievements, Wayne is also an actor, having appeared in popular British television shows such as Peaky Blinders and Coronation Street. Additionally, he is an accomplished writer and columnist, contributing to various publications and authoring several self-help books.

Despite his growing fame, Wayne remains grounded, regularly performing at both high-profile events and local community gatherings, where he continues to share his passion for music and giving back to the community.

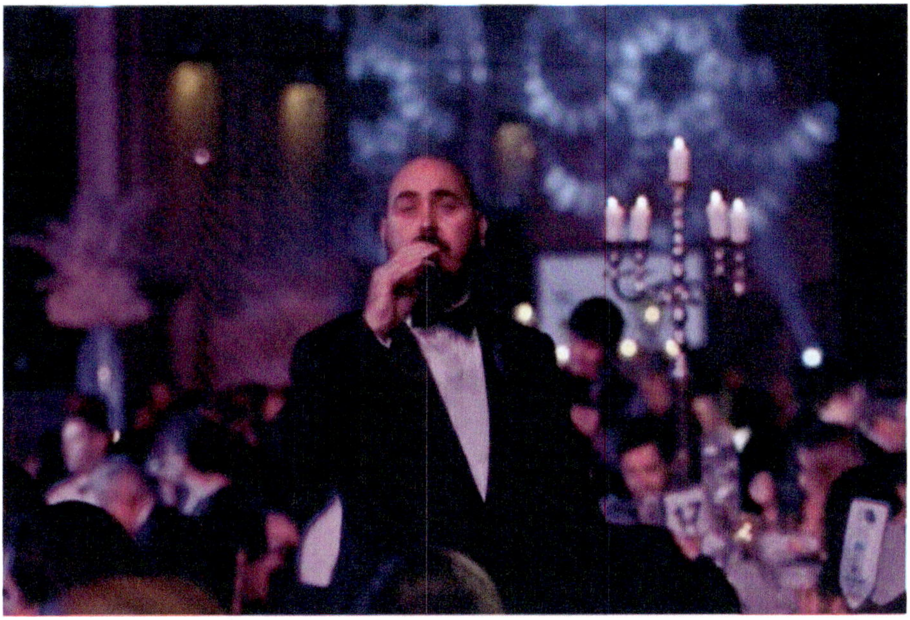

Printed in Great Britain
by Amazon